Learn

·ton Stre

D1433686

A SORT OF LIFE

OTHER BOOKS BY

GRAHAM GREENE

NOVELS

The Man Within
Stamboul Train
It's a Battlefield
England Made Me
A Gun for Sale
Brighton Rock
The Confidential Agent
The Power and the Glory
The Ministry of Fear
The Heart of the Matter
The Third Man
The End of the Affair
Loser Takes All
The Quiet American
Our Man in Havana
A Burnt-Out Case
The Comedians
Travels with my Aunt

SHORT STORIES

Twenty-One Stories
A Sense of Reality
May We Borrow Your Husband?

TRAVEL

Journey Without Maps
The Lawless Roads
In Search of a Character

ESSAYS

Collected Essays

PLAYS

The Living Room
The Potting Shed
The Complaisant Lover
Carving a Statue

A
SORT
OF
LIFE

Graham Greene

THE BODLEY HEAD
LONDON SYDNEY
TORONTO

© Graham Greene 1971
ISBN 0 370 00327 6
Printed and bound in Great Britain for
The Bodley Head Ltd
9 Bow Street, London WC2E 7AL
by William Clowes & Sons Ltd, Beccles
Set in Monotype Ehrhardt
First published 1971
Reprinted 1971

For the survivors,
Raymond Greene, Hugh Greene
and Elisabeth Dennys

Only robbers and gypsies say that one
must never return where one has once been.
Kierkegaard

An autobiography is only 'a sort of life'—it may contain less errors of fact than a biography, but it is of necessity even more selective: it begins later and it ends prematurely. If one cannot close a book of memories on the deathbed, any conclusion must be arbitrary, and I have preferred to finish this essay with the years of failure which followed the acceptance of my first novel. Failure too is a kind of death: the furniture sold, the drawers emptied, the removal van waiting like a hearse in the lane to take one to a less expensive destination. In another sense too a book like this can only be 'a sort of life', for in the course of sixty-six years I have spent almost as much time with imaginary characters as with real men and women. Indeed, though I have been fortunate in the number of my friends, I can remember no anecdotes of the famous or the notorious—the only stories which I faintly remember are the stories I have written.

And the motive for recording these scraps of the past? It is much the same motive that has made me a novelist: a desire to reduce a chaos of experience to some sort of order, and a hungry curiosity. We cannot love others, so the theologians teach, unless in some degree we can love ourselves, and curiosity too begins at home.

There is a fashion today among many of my contemporaries to treat the events of their past with irony. It is a legitimate method of self-defence. 'Look how absurd I was when I was young' forestalls cruel criticism, but it falsifies history. We were not Eminent Georgians. Those emotions were real when we felt them. Why should we be more ashamed of them than of the indifference of old age? I have tried, however unsuccessfully, to live again the follies and sentimentalities and exaggerations of the distant time, and to feel them, as I felt them then, without irony.

Chapter 1

I

If I had known it, the whole future must have lain all the time along those Berkhamsted streets. The High Street was wide as many a market square, but its broad dignity was abused after the first great war by the New Cinema under a green Moorish dome, tiny enough but it seemed to us then the height of pretentious luxury and dubious taste. My father, who was by that time headmaster of Berkhamsted School, once allowed his senior boys to go there for a special performance of the first *Tarzan* movie, under the false impression that it was an educational film of anthropological interest, and ever after he regarded the cinema with a sense of disillusion and suspicion. The High Street contained at 'our end' a half-timbered Tudor photographer's shop (from the windows the faces of the locals looked out in wedding groups, bouqueted and bemused like prize oxen) and the great flinty Norman church where the helmet of some old Duke of Cornwall hung unremarked on a pillar like a bowler hat in a hall. Below lay the Grand Junction canal with slow-moving painted barges and remote gypsy children, the watercress beds, the hillocks of the old castle surrounded by a dry moat full of cow-parsley (it had been built, so they said, by Chaucer, and in the reign of King Henry III it was besieged successfully by the French). The faint agreeable smell of coal dust blew up from the railway, and everywhere were those curious individual Berkhamsted faces which I feel I could recognize now anywhere in the world: pointed faces like the knaves on playing cards, with a slyness about the eyes, an unsuccessful cunning.

And then there remains to be set reluctantly on my personal map the School—part rosy Tudor, part hideous modern brick the colour of dolls'-house plaster hams—where the misery of life started, and the burial ground, long disused, which lay opposite our windows, separated from our flower-beds by an invisible line, so that every year the gardener would turn up a few scraps of human bone in remaking the herbaceous border. Further off to the north, on the green spaces of a map empty as Africa, lay the wastes of gorse and bracken of the great Common which extended to Ashridge Park, and to the south the small Brickhill Common and the park of Ashlyns, where I once saw a Jack in the Green covered with spring leaves, dancing cumbrously among his attendants like the devils I met later in Liberia.

Everything one was to become must have been there, for better or worse. One's future might have been prophesied from the shape of the houses as from the lines of the hand; one's evasions and deceits took their form from those other sly faces and from the hiding places in the garden, on the Common, in the hedgerows. Here in Berkhamsted was the first mould of which the shape was to be endlessly reproduced. For twenty years it was to be almost the only scene of happiness, misery, first love, the attempt to write, and I feel it would be strange if, through the workings of co-incidence, through the unconscious sources of action, through folly or wisdom, I were not brought back to die there in the place where everything was born.

At the far end of the long High Street was the village of Northchurch and an old inn, the Crooked Billet. The name, perhaps because of some event which had happened there and had left an ambiguous impression in my mind from veiled adult conversation, always had for me a sinister ring (in the inn I was sure travellers had been done to death), and this gave the whole Northchurch village an atmosphere of standing outside the pale: a region of danger where night-mare might easily become reality. We were never taken there for walks, though this could well have had a natural explana-tion, for why should any nurse endure the two-mile trudge along the High Street, past the town hall, past the new King's Road, up and down which the commuters streamed twice a day to the station with their little attaché cases, past Mrs Figg's toy-shop where the children would certainly want to linger, past the sinister stained glass windows of the dentist, along the market gardens, with everywhere that odd gritty smell blowing up from the coal yards and the coal barges?

There was another walk too which we never took when we were in charge of our old crotchety nurse or the nurse-maid, and that was the walk along the towing path by the canal. If a sinister atmosphere lay in my mind around the Crooked Billet, a sense of immediate danger was conveyed by the canal—the menace of insulting words from strange brutal canal workers with blackened faces like miners, with their gypsy wives and ragged children, at the sight of middle-class children carefully dressed and shepherded, and the danger too, as I believed, of death from drowning. *The Berkhamsted Gazette and Hemel Hempstead Observer* periodically printed the reports of inquests on those found drowned in the canal; the casualties among the barge children were reputed to be high, and the story that anyone who fell into a lock was beyond rescue was not contradicted in our imaginations by the lifebelt which hung on the wall of each lock-house. I cannot to this day peer down into a lock, down the sheer wet walls, without a sense of trepidation, and many of my early dreams were of death by drowning, of being drawn magnetically towards the water's edge. (So strong did these dreams become in my adolescent years that they affected my waking life, and the margin of a pond or a river would attract my feet, just as a fast car can hypnotize a pedestrian on an otherwise empty road.)

2

The first thing I remember is sitting in a pram at the top of a hill with a dead dog lying at my feet. It was close by the fields which were later to become, thanks to the beneficence of my rich Uncle Edward—known for mysterious reasons as Eppy—the playing-fields of Berkhamsted School, for even the geography of the little town was influenced by the two big families of Greenes (seventeen Greenes resident in one small place would seem even today an unduly high proportion of the population, and at holiday times the Greenes could nearly reach a quarter of a century). The dog, as I know now, was a pug owned by my elder sister. It had been run over—by a horse-carriage?—and killed and the nurse thought it convenient to bring the cadaver home this way. The memory may well be a true one, as my mother once told me how surprised she had been months later by some reference which I made to the 'poor dog'; they were almost the first words I had spoken.

In all these early years I am uncertain what is genuinely remembered. For example I think I can remember a toy motor-car, which now surely—a 1908 vintage toy—might be worthy of a sale at Sotheby's, but since it appears in a photograph of myself and my brother Raymond, this may not be a true memory. My age then was about four, and I wore a pinafore and had fair curls falling around the neck. My elder brother with a proper masculine haircut, an adult of seven, stares fearlessly towards the box-camera, like a future mountaineer of Kamet and Everest, while I still have the ambiguity of undetermined sex.

As children we used to go down to the drawing-room for about an hour after tea, from 5.30 to 6.30, to play with our mother, and I remember the fear I felt that my mother would read us a story about some children who were sent into a forest by a wicked uncle to be murdered, but the murderer repented and left them to die of exposure and afterwards the birds covered their bodies with leaves. I dreaded the story because I was afraid of weeping. I would infinitely have preferred quick murder to the long drawn-out pathos of their end. My tear-ducts in childhood, and indeed for many years later, worked far too easily, and even today I sometimes slink shame-faced from a cinema at some happy ending that moves me by its incredibility. (Life isn't like that. Of such courage and such fidelity we dream only, but in my distress I wish them true.)

As I approach school-age the memories thicken. One vivid memory (I was probably about five) was of passing with my nurse the old alms-houses which leant against each other near the Grand Junction canal. There was a crowd outside one of the little houses and a man broke away and ran into the house. I was told that he was going to cut his throat, nobody followed him, everybody, including my nurse and I, stood outside waiting, but I never learnt whether he succeeded. *The Berkhamsted Gazette* would have informed me, but I couldn't yet read.*

Of all my first six years I have only such random memories as these and I cannot be sure of the time-sequence. They are significant for me because they remain, the stray symbols of a dream after the story has sunk back into the unconscious, and they cry for rescue like the survivors of a shipwreck.

There was a particular kind of wheaten biscuit with a very pale pure unsweetened flavour—I am reminded now of the Host—which only my mother had the right to eat. They

* Perhaps there is an understandable failure of memory here, for my brother Raymond writes to me: 'You did in fact see the man cut his throat, standing by a first floor window, or the nurse may have obstructed your view. Anyway he succeeded.'

were kept in a special biscuit-tin in her bedroom and sometimes as a favour I was given one to eat dipped in milk. I associate my mother with a remoteness, which I did not at all resent, and with a smell of eau-de-cologne. If I could have tasted her I am sure she would have tasted of wheaten biscuits. She paid occasional state visits to the nursery in the School House, a large confused room which looked out on the flint church and the old cemetery, with toy cupboards and bookshelves and a big wooden rocking-horse with wicked eyes and one large comfortable wicker-chair for the nurse beside the steel fireguard, and my mother gained in my eyes great dignity from her superintendence of the linen-cupboard, where a frightening witch lurked, but of that later. The wheaten biscuit remains for me a symbol of her cool puritan beauty—she seemed to eliminate all confusion, to recognize the good from the bad and choose the good, though where her family was concerned in later years she noticed only the good. If one of us had committed murder she would, I am sure, have blamed the victim. When she was in an untroubled coma before death and I was watching by her bed, her long white plantagenet face reminded me of a crusader on a tomb. It seemed the right peaceful end for the tall calm beautiful girl standing in a punt in a long skirt with a tiny belted waist and wearing a straw boater whom I had seen in the family album.

An unpleasant memory of those years is of a tin jerry full of blood: I was feeling horribly sick, for I had just had my adenoids out and my tonsils cut. The operation had been done at home. For thirty years after that the sight of blood worried and sickened me, so that sometimes I fainted at the mere description of an accident. In the blitz, before I encountered the first wounded, I was afraid of what my reaction might be until I found that fear and the necessity of action conquered the nausea.

Our home until I reached the age of six was a house called St John's, one of the boarding-houses of Berkhamsted School. My father was housemaster there. When he became the headmaster in 1910 we removed to the School House, but I went back to St John's as a boarder at thirteen and most of my memories of the house (and very unhappy ones they are) date back to that time. Before that first climacteric I remember of St John's only the extra piece of garden we had across the road, where on special days in summer we would go and play with the exciting sense of travelling abroad. There was a summer-house there (no such thing existed on the every-day side), and the garden was built up high above the road so that I couldn't see over the bushes to my home which might have been a hundred miles away. It was my first experience of foreign travel. Later I used to think of the two gardens as resembling England and France with the Channel between, although I had never been to France—England for every day and France for holidays.

At the far end of Berkhamsted at the Hall, the great house of the town, lived the family of Greene cousins. The mother was German and the whole family had an intimidatingly exotic air, for many of them had been born in Brazil near Santos, on a *fazenda* which was also the name of the coffee we drank. There were six children, the same number as in our family, and in ages they were inserted between us, our family starting first, as though my uncle, who was the younger brother, had suffered from a competitive spirit and wanted to catch my father up. My own particular friend was Tooter, though it was with his younger sister Barbara that I was years later to make the rather foolhardy journey through Liberia which I have described in *Journey Without Maps*.

My uncle's children were the rich Greenes and we were regarded as the intellectual Greenes. We would visit them on Christmas Eve for the Christmas tree, my elder siblings staying for dinner. I used to be embarrassed by the carols in German round the tree because I was afraid I might be expected to sing too. The whole affair in our eyes seemed rather Teutonic, for to us the eve of Christmas had no significance at all. Christmas only began the next morning with the crunchy feel of a heavy stocking lying across the toes and a slight feeling of nausea, due to excitement, which bore the family name of a 'Narcissus tummy-ache'. I don't remember any Christmas tree in our house, and mistletoe was an embarrassing joke played by our elders. Kissing had no appeal, and I kept well away from the mistletoe if anyone else were around.

On Christmas Eve, at the Hall, the children all had their presents laid on separate tables which were identified by names on cards. I remember being bitterly disappointed once when an adult present, a leather writing-case, on my table, turned out to be there in error: it was intended for my uncle, who bore the same name and who was the Permanent

Secretary of the Admiralty and a Knight of the Bath—a title which I found impressive and not funny at all.

Very remote my uncle Graham seemed, and the more important for his dryness and his taciturnity and the glasses which dangled over his waistcoat on a broad black ribbon. Even today I find it difficult to think of him as a little boy riding to school in Cambridge on a donkey. His speech was all 'ehs' and 'ahs'. Perhaps he felt ill at ease with anyone but a civil servant. He died unmarried in 1950 at his home in Harston at the age of ninety-three, looked after by his two old sisters, Helen and Polly, both in their eighties. At the age of eighty-nine he fell under a tube train owing to failing eyesight on his way to attend a sub-committee of the Committee of Imperial Defence which was to discuss the import of reindeer into the north of Scotland. He lay, quiet and self-possessed, beside the live rail while the train moved back and it was found that he had only bruised a rib. With difficulty he was persuaded to return to Harston. There, when he was ninety-one, he fell out of a tree (he was pruning the branches) and for a while he had to take to his bed, but a more humdrum accident proved the fatal one, a year later, when he tripped over a chair on the lawn. He survived quite a while even then, though bed-ridden, having *The Times* leaders read to him every morning, and the first sign of his approaching end was when my old aunts while undressing him removed a toe with his socks. He was a remarkable man, if we had only known it. Having been drummed out of the Admiralty after Jutland by Lloyd George and the Northcliffe Press, he joined his friend

Winston Churchill at the Ministry of Munitions. Only recently in a volume of the *Dictionary of National Biography* did I learn of his connexion with the world of James Bond— he was one of the founders of Naval Intelligence. Carson told how 'I met Churchill in the prime minister's room and congratulated him on his knowledge of men. "What do you mean?" said Lloyd George. "Well," I said, "Winston has the wisdom to choose for a much bigger job the man you dismissed from the Admiralty".'

My uncle lived in a big house at Harston in Cambridge-shire, and as children we would go there for the summer holidays, though later my elders went away to the Lake District to climb and I was left with my mother and the baby Hugh. (Finally my sister Molly fell off a mountain and got married to the man who photographed her fall—perhaps she admired his presence of mind.)

Harston House was—at least in part—a lovely William-and-Mary house, and it had a large old-fashioned garden very suited to hide-and-seek, with an orchard, a stream and a big pond containing an island, and there was a fountain on the front lawn. We would fix a cup to the handle of a walk-ing stick, and the water so obtained tasted very cold and very pure. The fountain was about two feet deep and a yard across. Once my elder brother Raymond fell in at the age of three, and when asked how he had got out he replied with bravura, 'I struck out for the shore.' The smell of apples seemed to fall everywhere over the garden and the smell of box hedges, and there was a buzz of bees in the hot summer weather. I remember the funeral of a dead bird which was coffined in a Price's night-light box. My elders, Herbert and Molly and Raymond, buried him in what was called the Shady Walk. I was only a minor mourner, being the youngest, too young and unimportant to be priest or grave-digger or chorister.

My uncle was never there when we were. He stayed safely away from any family turbulence in his bachelor flat off Hanover Square. I had a very possessive feeling for the great rambling garden, and I was furious one year when my mother invited another small boy called Harker, the son of the school doctor, to share my summer there. I treated him as a pariah, I wouldn't play with him, I would hardly speak to him. I never showed him how to get water from the fountain, and I knew hiding places that he would never find, so that he was left ambling aimlessly without a companion, bored sometimes to tears. The experience of that terrible long August was never repeated and thereafter I was allowed to stay alone.

It was at Harston I quite suddenly found that I could read—the book was *Dixon Brett, Detective*. I didn't want anyone to know of my discovery, so I read only in secret, in a remote attic, but my mother must have spotted what I was at all the same, for she gave me Ballantyne's *Coral Island* for the train journey home—always an interminable journey with the long wait between trains at Bletchley. I still wouldn't admit my new talent, and I stared at the only illustration all the way to the junction. No wonder it so impressed itself on my memory that I can see with my mind's eye today the group of children posed on the rocks.

I think I feared that reading represented the entrance to the Preparatory School (I went through the grim portal a few weeks before my eighth birthday), or perhaps I disliked the sense of patronage which I always detected when I was praised for something others did quite naturally. Only a few years ago at an Edinburgh ceremonial my memory was confirmed by Doctor Dover Wilson, the Shakespearian scholar, who told me that my parents often spoke to him of the difficulty they found in teaching me to read. I detested that absurd book with the engravings which now seem so charming, *Reading Without Tears*. How could I be interested in a cat who sat on a mat? I couldn't identify with a cat. Dixon Brett was quite another matter, and he had a boy assistant, who might easily, I thought, have been myself.

I particularly resented my father's interest. How could a grown man, I argued, feel any concern for what happened on a child's walk? To be praised was agony—I would crawl immediately under the nearest table. Until I had grown up I think my only real moments of affection for my father were when he made frog-noises with his palms, or played Fly Away, Jack, Fly Away, Jill, with a piece of sticking-plaster on his finger, or made me blow open the lid of his watch. Only when I had children of my own did I realize how his interest in my doings had been genuine, and only then I discovered a buried love and sorrow for him, which emerges today from time to time in dreams.

I think that my parents' was a very loving marriage; how far any marriage is happy is another matter and beyond an outsider's knowledge. Happiness can be ruined by children, by financial anxieties, by so many secret things: love too can be ruined, but I think their love withstood the pressure of six children and great anxieties. I was in Sierra Leone, running ineffectually a one-man office of the Secret Service, when my father died in 1943. The news came in two telegrams delivered in the wrong order—the first told me of his death—the second an hour later of his serious illness. Suddenly, between the secret reports to be coded and decoded, I unexpectedly felt misery and remorse, remembering how as a young man I had deliberately set out to shock his ideas which had been unflinchingly liberal in politics and gently conservative in morals. I had a Mass said for him by Father Mackie, the Irish priest in Freetown. I thought that if my father could know he would regard the gesture with his accustomed liberality and kindly amusement—he had never disputed by so much as a word my decision to become a Catholic. At least I felt sure that my method of payment would have pleased him. The priest asked me for a sack of rice for his poor African parishioners, for rice was scarce and severely rationed, and through my friendship with the Commissioner of Police I was able to buy one clandestinely.

Both parents have known someone the children have never known. My father had known the tall girl with the tiny waist wearing a boater, and my mother the young dandyish man who appeared in a tinted Oxford photograph on their bathroom wall, with a well-trimmed moustache, wearing evening dress with a blue waistcoat. More than ten years after his death my mother wrote to me. She had broken her hip and she had dreamt unhappily that my father had not come to see her in hospital or even written to her and she couldn't understand it. Now, even when she was awake, she felt unhappy because of his silence. Oddly enough I too had dreamt of him a few days before. My mother and I were driving in a car and at a turn in the road my father had signalled to us, and when we stopped he came running to catch us up. He was happy, he had a joyful smile as he climbed into the back of the car, for he had been let out of hospital that morning. I wrote to my mother that perhaps there was some truth in the idea of purgatory, and this was the moment of release.

For me this dream was the end of a series which had recurred over the years after his death. In them my father was always shut away in hospital out of touch with his wife and children—though sometimes he returned home on a visit, a silent solitary man, not really cured, who would have to go back again into exile. The dreams remain vivid even today, so that sometimes it is an effort for me to realize that there was no hospital, no separation, and that he lived with my mother till he died. In his last years he had diabetes and always beside her place at table there stood a weighing-machine to measure his diet, and it was she who daily gave him his injections of insulin. There was no truth at all in the idea of his loneliness and unhappiness, but perhaps the dreams show that I loved him more than I knew.

The only separation that really existed was from his children. As a headmaster he was even more distant than our aloof mother. At the Easter holidays we would go to the seaside at Littlehampton, travelling with our mother and nurse

[25]

in a reserved third-class compartment with a hamper-lunch, but my father wisely would always come down alone a few days later second-class. Sometimes he took a winter holiday alone in Egypt or in France or Italy with a friend, Mr George, a clergyman and headmaster. They remained very formal through all the years, calling each other by their surnames, though naturally George has a less formal sound than Greene. I think their holidays were more intellectual than convivial, for I remember my father naming some place in France visited many years before and saying to his friend, 'You remember, George, that was where we drank a bottle of wine.' Once—it was in Naples—they had a curious encounter. A stranger hearing them speak in English asked whether he might join them over their coffee. There was something familiar and to them vaguely disagreeable about his face, but he kept them charmed by his wit for more than an hour before he said goodbye. They didn't exchange names even at parting and he left them to pay for his drink which was certainly not coffee. It was some while before they realized in whose company they had been. The stranger was Oscar Wilde, who not very long before had been released from prison. 'Think,' my father would always conclude his story, 'how lonely he must have been to have expended so much time and wit on a couple of schoolmasters on holiday.' It never occurred to him that Wilde was paying for his drink in the only currency he had.*

* I think this encounter must have been during the Christmas holidays of 1897–8 when his friend Bosie had departed and Wilde wrote of 'ill-health, loneliness and general *ennui* with a tragi-comedy of an existence'.

My mother's remoteness, her wonderful lack of the possessive instinct, was made much easier for her to achieve by the presence of Nanny, an old woman who came first to look after my elder sister, some thirteen years before these memories begin, and by a long succession of nursery-maids (who never endured very long, for perhaps they represented a threat to Nanny's future). I remember her bent over my bath with her white hair in a bun, holding a sponge. Her temper deteriorated before she retired on a pension, but I never remember being afraid of her, only impressed by that white bun of age.

Before I was old enough to be taken on these holidays to Littlehampton, when all I knew of the sea was from the gossip of my elders, I used to assume that a pile of sand in a timber yard by the canal bank at Berkhamsted was the sea-side; it seemed quite unremarkable to me, and I saw no reason to envy my brothers and sister. Indeed I was very content in those days to remain in one place (a contentment which I envy now). On the occasion of King George V's coronation, when I was six, I was given the choice of going to London with my parents and the three elder children to seats procured for them by my uncle Graham or of watching the local Berkhamsted procession in the company of my maiden aunt Maud who lived in the town. The more economical alternative carried with it the right to choose a toy from the toy-shop, and to the relief of my parents I chose to stay.*

* I think my decision was the right one. This is how my brother Raymond, who was ten, described the great day: 'We got up at 4.15 in

[27]

The toy I chose was a table croquet-set, and I remember with irritation how difficult it was to make the hooked hoops stand straight on a tablecloth. In the local procession somebody rode in armour on a horse, impersonating probably the Duke of Cornwall, and this recalled the picture of a knight in a big bound volume of some girls' magazine in the dining-room. (Later I loved *Ivanhoe* and Maurice Hewlett's *The Forest Lovers* and the first stories I tried to write were of the Middle Ages.) The toy-shop was kept by the old woman called Figg in the High Street. One climbed down a few steps into something like a crowded cabin, where on bunk over bunk lay the long narrow boxes of Britain's toy soldiers, quite inexpensive in those days, in an amazing variety which recalled all the imperial wars of the past century: Sepoys and Zulus and Boers and Russians and French. From memories of those first six years I have a general impression of tranquillity and happiness, and the world held enormous interest, even though I disappointed my mother on my first visit to the Zoo by sitting down and saying, 'I'm tired. I want to go home.'

the morning and had breakfast. At Euston we took a cab and drove to Trafalgar Square. Then we couldn't go on as it was such a crowd, but at last we got to the Admiralty. We waited about two hours and then the procession came by. Soldiers first, then the state carriages with dukes in ermine with coronets. Then more soldiers and state carriages and then the Royal coach and the King with his crown on. Then came more soldiers etc. After dinner it came by again and just as the crown was put on the King's head, the street lamps lighted, 41 guns fired and then we came home and we were awfully tired.' Oh, the fatigues of childhood never to be equalled till old age.

There were terrors, too, of course, but they would have been terrors at any age. I distinguish here between terror and fear. From terror one escapes screaming, but fear has an odd seduction. Fear and the sense of sex are linked in secret conspiracy, but terror is a sickness like hate.

I inherited from my mother a blinding terror of birds and bats. Even today I loathe the touch of feathers, and I remember how one night at Harston a bat came into my bedroom from one of the great trees on the lawn outside. I saw it poke its furry nose first around the curtains and wait to be observed. Next night I was allowed to keep the window shut, but a bat—I was sure it was the same one—then came down the chimney. I shrieked with my head under the sheet, until my brother Raymond came and caught it in a butterfly net.*

Another recurring terror was of the house catching fire at night and I associate it with sticky coloured plates in the *Boys' Own Paper* recording the exploits of heroic firemen. There always seemed to be fires in those days, and yet I never actually saw a fire until I witnessed too many of them in the winter of 1940–41. I think it was later, when I was seven, menaced by the approach of school and a new sort of life, that I was terrified by a witch who would lurk at night on the nursery landing by the linen-cupboard. After a long

* The fear of bats remains. I had to steel myself later in Angkor Wat to pass a damaged bat flapping on the floor of a passage, while up in the pineapple towers one could see small men on ropes gathering the bats' dung. In those days there were Vietminh ambushes around Angkor, but I would have preferred an ambush to that dying bat.

[29]

series of nightmares when the witch would leap on my back and dig long mandarin finger-nails into my shoulders, I dreamt I turned on her and fought back and after that she never again appeared in sleep.

Dreams have always had an importance for me: 'the finest entertainment known and given rag cheap'. Two novels and several short stories have emerged from my dreams, and sometimes I have had hints of what is called by the difficult name of extra-sensory perception. On the April night of the *Titanic* disaster, when I was five and it was Easter holiday time in Littlehampton, I dreamt of a ship-wreck. One image of the dream has remained with me for more than sixty years: a man in oilskins bent double beside a companion-way under the blow of a great wave. Again in 1921 I wrote home from my psycho-analyst's: 'A night or two ago I had a shipwreck dream, the ship I was on going down in the Irish Sea. I didn't think anything about it. We don't have papers here as the usual thing, and it was not till yesterday, looking at an old paper, I saw about the sinking of the *Rowan* in the Irish Sea. I looked at my dream diary and found that my dream had been Saturday night. The accident had happened just after Saturday midnight.' Again in 1944 I dreamed of a V.1 missile some weeks before the first attack. It passed horizontally across the sky flaming at the tail in the very form it was to take.

3

Memory is like a long broken night. As I write, it is as though I am waking from sleep continually to grasp at an image which I hope may drag in its wake a whole intact dream, but the fragments remain fragments, the complete story always escapes.

I must have been still under six years old when we all waited through a sunny afternoon in the St John's garden—on the English side of the road—for the chance of seeing Blériot making his London to Manchester flight, but he never passed overhead—it was a long afternoon wasted, when we might have been across the Channel in France, in the holiday-garden.

I hated the very idea of children's parties. They were a threat that one day I might have to put to practical use my dancing lessons, of which I can only remember the black shiny shoes with the snappy elastic and the walk down King's Road, between the red-brick villas on winter evenings, holding someone's hand for fear of slipping. The only children's party I can actually remember was up near Berkhamsted Common in a big strange house, where I never went again; a Chinese amah asked me if I wanted to make water and I did not understand her, so that always afterwards I thought of it as a Chinese expression. Many years later I wrote a short story about a children's party, and another about dancing lessons, and perhaps there are memories concealed in them too.

I have an impression my father used to smack me as a

2+S.O.L.   [31]

child, though I can remember only one specific beating at a later age, perhaps because it woke a sexual interest in me. Once I called my maiden aunt Maud a bugger and she reported it to my father, who pulled me out from under a table and demanded an apology which I was unwilling to give, not knowing what my offence was. Indeed I never meant to offend her. I was closer to her perhaps than to any other of my numerous aunts, most of them officially maiden —Helen who ran a school of Swedish gymnastics and had passionate women friendships, dear muddle-headed Polly who lived at Harston and painted bad pictures and taught Gwen Raverat to draw and wrote ambitious plays for the village institute (the whole conflict between Christianity and Paganism in Northumbria she managed to contain in a one-act piece with fifty characters), the beautiful mysteriously gay Nora (whom we knew as Nono), Alice, the progressive, who ran a school in South Africa and was a friend of General Smuts and Olive Schreiner, Madge, an aunt-by-marriage, the pretty daughter of the Irish poet Doctor Todhunter— she sang songs about 'Away with the gipsies oh' in pre-Raphaelite gowns from Liberty's.

And somehow left out, I think, of all the children's memories except as a figure in the remote background of the sunny garden—one had to peer to see her closer—there was Florence, who lived in her own cottage at Harston. Harston had been colonized by the Greenes almost as effectively as Berkhamsted or, as I was to discover later, St Kitts. The Greenes seemed to move as a tribe like the Bantus, taking possession. Helen, Polly, Alice and Florence were all paternal Greenes, and Florence was the only girl to marry, but as she had no children she returned to the tribe. I remember her as a thin peaky old lady, her face, which had perhaps been beautiful, hidden behind a spotted veil, tied like Queen Alexandra's under the chin. She had none of the gaiety, fantasy and silliness of Polly; she wasn't brusque and masculine like Helen and Alice. She hadn't a family voice at all that one could recognize. It was as though her loss of virginity kept her apart from all the other Greene aunts— she was only Mrs Phillips, the widow of a county schoolmaster. And yet before she married she had been the most romantic of them all. At eighteen she fell in love with a young sailor who wanted to leave the navy and emigrate with her to the wilder parts of Australia, but the wisdom of older relations prevailed. Otherwise Australia might have been colonized too. Four years later a rich brewer in Lincoln wanted to marry her and gave her the *Life of Charles Kingsley*. He was a poor substitute for the young sailor and nothing came of that. There was a Mr Rust, but no one ever knew which of the sisters he had an eye on, so Florence finally settled for Mr Phillips, the schoolmaster. He kept a little monkey who ate oranges, dividing them meticulously, peeled paper off the walls, and put his arms tenderly round Mr Phillips' neck. Would Mr Phillips without the monkey have been enough? Strangely, as an old lady, one thought of Aunt Florence as being always on a visit, from remoter regions even than Alice, perhaps from Australia.

Maud, my mother's sister, was 'the poor relation' who lived alone in a little house near the school and was made use of by my mother as a fourth at bridge and to take me as a convalescent child to Brighton. She vexed my mother by a nervous trick of yawning and sighing at frequent intervals which was apt to discourage her partner, if he was meeting her for the first time. Nothing that happened in Berkhamsted escaped her eye: she was a walking news-letter, and this too was a cause of irritation to my mother, who, perhaps, thought that as the headmaster's wife she was in danger of figuring in the headlines. In later life I loved my aunt for this very quality, and would make journeys from London to have tea with her and hear the latest gossip of Berkhamsted. The headmaster, when he was no longer a Greene, was fair game, and one in particular caused a good deal of sexual scandal at which my aunt scarcely pretended to be shocked. Her ear was very close to the ground. Once I arrived with my brother Hugh unannounced, walking directly from the railway station five minutes away. She opened the door to us, saying, 'When I heard you were in Berkhamsted I put on the kettle for tea.'

It was after I was six and we had all moved to the School House, but before I went to school, that I began regularly to steal currants and sultanas out of the big biscuit-tins in the School House store-room, stuff my pockets full with them, currants in the left, sultanas in the right, and feast on them secretly in the garden. The meal ended always with a sensation of nausea, but to be secure from detection I had to finish them all, even the strays which had picked up fluff from the seams of the pockets. There is a charm in improvised eating which a regular meal lacks, and there was a glamour never to be recaptured in secret picnics on long sunny mornings on the roof of the Hall, our uncle's big house. No stone of it now remains, a building estate has swallowed all—the lawns, the trees, the stables and the meadows, which were to be the scenery of my calf-love. When I see a performance of *The Cherry Orchard* today, it is on that estate I hear the axes falling. I would sit up there with my cousin Tooter, consuming sweets bought with our weekly pocket money (which was twopence, I think) and discussing possible futures—as a midshipman in the Navy or an Antarctic explorer—none of them to be realized, while we watched the oblivious figures in the yard and the stables below from our godlike secrecy and security. The sweets I remember best were white and tubular, much thinner than any cigarette, filled with a dark chocolate filling. If I found one now I am sure that it would have the taste of hope.

A smell which comes back from those years was the smell of a breakfast food which I didn't like. The same smell I noticed later from sacks of grain outside a corn chandler's, and curiously it was the smell too of my carriers' sweat in Liberia in 1935, and yet there in the damp heat and the strangeness, as they lay close around me at night for fear of cannibals, I enjoyed the smell: it had become the smell of Africa.

Post-six too are my memories of being ill—it happened often, but only the dentist left unhappy memories. Till now I have never suffered greater pain than I did then. I remember rolling on the drawing-room floor in agony from an exposed nerve. I don't think he was a very good dentist, and for years after I had left his care I would avoid walking, on the way to Northchurch and the Crooked Billet, past his house and the stained glass window representing the Laughing Cavalier which hid the chair of torture. Later I resented the fact that my parents used to visit a dentist in London—Mr Crick, I felt sure, was as painless as he was expensive.

But of my other ailments I retain only a sense of peaceful darkness, of endless time, of privacy, a night-light burning, and of books bought by my mother for me to read, sometimes ones that bored me, like *The Man-eaters of Tsavo*. Apart from the tonsil operation I can remember only one unhappy illness—the first attack of hay-fever after playing in a haystack with my cousins. Nobody knew what it was, and I seemed to lie awake coughing and gasping for breath all night long. No later attack was so severe, and even the pains of pleurisy, which I had later, were more easily bearable and less frightening; perhaps it was during that night I evolved my fear of drowning—I was able to imagine the lungs filling with water.

There are two stray scatological memories of the time. For some reason—it can only have been a convalescence—I found myself at Littlehampton alone with Nora, my mother's favourite sister, so much gayer, more elegant and popular than poor Maud, who once burst into tears when my German aunt spoke of the beautiful hair she possessed when she was young. I was too embarrassed by her elegance to tell my aunt that I wanted to go to the lavatory and I fouled my knickers. At six too I made, perhaps it was on the same occasion, a coloured drawing of a bit of shit for the *School House Gazette*, a periodical in manuscript edited by my eldest brother Herbert (I had the rank of office boy). My memory tells me that the drawing was included because it was taken for a cigar, and I was a little annoyed at the misunderstanding, though I put nobody right, and yet recently I have searched in vain for my painting in the pages of the *Gazette*—perhaps the true meaning of it was understood after all.

Apart from the corpse of my sister's pug at the bottom of my pram, the only domestic animal I can remember was a Pekinese called Bicki which also belonged to Molly, for she was the only one of us ever allowed to own a dog. We in the nursery shared a succession of canaries (one broke a blood vessel singing too loud and long), and I once owned two white mice, but when one ate the other and then died of loneliness, I was falsely accused of having starved them, so they were never replaced. My brother Herbert (but that was a long while after) brought home a baby pig which he had won at a fair and lodged it in his bedroom for the night. On the floor below, unable to sleep, I had the strong impression that he was kicking a football around—he was the athlete of the family. The pig was not allowed to stay.

The Pekinese arrived nailed down in a box. It was in a savage temper after a long railway journey, and it remained consistently unamiable towards my sister who owned it and bit her on many occasions. Bicki and I got on well together. Once it was lost after a walk, the police were warned, and

[37]

eventually many hours later, when the streets of Berkhamsted had been well scoured and messages sent to Boxmoor and Hemel Hempstead and Chesham, it was found asleep under my bed. My mother was always unfavourably disposed towards dogs, until many years later she became attached to a mongrel of my own called Paddy, and after Bicki had bitten the baby Hugh it was sold quickly into another captivity.

The toy I remember most clearly was a fort. It was given me on my seventh birthday. It arrived dismantled, and I stuck the portcullis and walls and towers on to green cliffs by nails which fitted into holes. It was more like a medieval castle than the forts of Liège and Verdun which were soon to be so important in our lives and it was a little unsuitable for the Zulus who sometimes guarded it.

The games we played were: *French and English*. This was a garden game of conflict, but I can remember none of the rules which must have dated back to the Napoleonic wars. It was played by Charlotte Brontë in her childhood.

Hunt the Thimble. A special treat in the drawing-room when there were aunts and uncles about. At Christmas there was always an enormous number of Greene aunts and uncles, since my mother and father were first cousins of the same name, and a great many of them were unmarried and available.

Tom Tiddler's Ground. Played in the garden on the croquet lawn. A game of trespass. 'Here I come on Tom Tiddler's Ground, picking up gold and silver . . .'

The Ocean is Agitated. This was played on Christmas Day when the cousins came to tea. It was a kind of musical chairs.

One person promenaded round the circle calling out the name of a fish which had then to rise and follow. 'The ocean is agitated by a shrimp . . . by a shark . . . by a sardine' and finally 'The ocean is agitated by all the fish'. Then came 'The ocean is calm' and there was a scramble for chairs. I didn't care for this game. Even at an early age I found the chant ridiculous.

Hide-and-Seek in the Dark. This was a game containing the agreeable ingredient of fear, and we played it on the ground floor and first floor of the School House with all the lights out and in the big school hall during the holidays.

Hunt the Slipper. We played this rarely, but always at Christmas.

Musical Chairs. This was a ritual part of the Christmas Day tea-party, when the rich Greenes joined us from the Hall. On such occasions we would play in the old school hall, and I don't think anyone enjoyed it except perhaps the aunts and uncles.

General Post. Played on the same occasion, and with as little pleasure. Party games never seemed like real games (which were games without adults). They were obligations like going to church.

There were Charades, too, and Dumb Crambo, a kind of charade without dialogue, and a game called Clumps, which had been played in my father's childhood.

I have the impression that such games are becoming as obsolete as the street games described by Norman Douglas. Certainly I played none of them with my own children, for games like this demand a large family.

2* [39]

There was a real game too, not a party game, played in the old school hall and invented by my eldest brother Herbert, who was always of an adventurous character until he was changed by the continual and sometimes shameful failures of his adult life. We divided into sides and each side started from opposite ends of the hall. The lights had been turned out and one side must reach the opposite wall in the darkness without being caught. Benches had been piled on benches as obstacles. We listened with agreeably tense nerves for the creak of a board, scanned the blackness ahead, and felt our slow way, hands outstretched. I imagined myself a *franc-tireur* of the 1870 war of which I had read in a book of Henty's. War was still romantic, and every summer Herbert organized all-day manoeuvres with our cousins in the country lanes and fields behind the Hall. We carried sandwiches and ginger beer in bottles with glass marble stoppers, and the object of one side was to penetrate unseen to the stables and capture them. Scouting behind hedges, crawling along ditches, making heroic forays across an open space, one experienced the first hint of sexual interest for the enemy—the girl on sentry duty in the stable yard.

There was one entertainment I was not allowed to attend until I was much older. It was given, whenever he visited my parents at Berkhamsted, by an old clergyman called Canon Baldwin, who held the living at Harston. He recited the more grisly scenes from Shakespeare, in the dark of the drawing-room, taking all the parts himself: male and female. Sometimes, listening from a discreet distance in the hall outside, I heard muffled gurgles, chokes and screams, as

Duncan lay laced with his golden blood or Desdemona strangled. They were tense occasions for my parents, as a single cough from one of the privileged guests would stop the Canon in mid-speech and he would call angrily, like Hamlet's uncle, for lights. Perhaps it was not surprising that his daughter married Doctor Dover Wilson.

The Canon and my father were great chess-players. My father played for his county by correspondence, but he admitted that the Canon was the better man. The Canon would sometimes take my father for a walk up to the Common and play chess with him on the way. 'I open with Queen's Pawn Two,' he would say, and my father would make the appropriate response, but after about ten moves he lost his sense of the board, and the Canon would announce triumphantly and irrefutably, 'Checkmate.'

Chapter 2

I

Some time in 1910, when my father became headmaster, we removed from St John's (down the road into the High Street, turn left into Castle Street by the Norman church) to the School House, and that remained our home until my father's retirement in the twenties. The new things which most impressed me were the long path from the street to the front door, on the right the red-brick Tudor school hall and on the left, divided from me only by a flower-bed, the old disused churchyard. There was a white cat which used to sit on the tombstones and it was said by my father to be the ghost of a notorious absentee headmaster in the eighteenth century. When I was sixteen I sat on a gravestone with Peter Quennell and we both read aloud to each other from *The Yellow Book* with a sense of daring and decadence.

At the end of the long path, beyond the house, one reached the tennis-court, and beside the tennis-court was a small flower-garden with a pond full of tadpoles, and a buddleia which in summer swarmed with peacock butterflies. One of my early memories is of catching near the buddleia a female orange-tip which they told me was a very rare specimen, much rarer than the male. After I caught a butterfly I would put it in a poison-bottle, but a scruple always inhibited me from pinning it out in a case as my elders did, so the corpses soon became brittle and from frequent examination fell to powder, and then I threw them away. I wasn't scared of butterflies, but I was deeply afraid of moths—something about their hairy bodies terrified me. I fear them still and I am unhappy with one in the room until I have killed it. Beyond the buddleias lay two greenhouses at right-angles: in the small one were only potplants, geraniums and the like, but in the larger were plants of importance, orchids, which my father brought back from sales in London, and green grapes, and there was a deckchair in which my father at leisure moments would sit smoking a pipe and blowing smoke over the grapes to kill greenflies. There were very strict rules about never leaving a door open. I had the impression that the least drop in temperature brought instant death, and indeed I was not far from the truth. Once the gardener, who had the misleadingly responsible name of Charge, got tight and forgot to stoke the stove in the orchid house. All the orchids died including one for which my father had refused three hundred pounds—the equivalent of several thousand pounds today. It must have been a severe blow as it would be for me to have the manuscript of a story carelessly destroyed, but my elder brother cannot remember him even mentioning the matter, nor was the gardener sacked.

Through a gateway by the smaller greenhouse one passed to the croquet lawn, where at the far end were apple trees and a revolving shelter which figured in my first truancy. I don't clearly remember whether it was at this period I tried very hard to kill my brother Raymond by hitting him over the head with a croquet mallet, but I think this violent outbreak came later when I shared a room with him and we woke every morning to a quarrel. Now I shared a room uncomfortably with the baby Hugh, who cried at night and kept me awake.

Walking across the croquet lawn (what a vast estate the whole place seems to me now, when I live, like most of my contemporaries, an apartment-life between bedroom and sitting-room), one came to a wooden fence which separated it from the kitchen-garden and a forest of raspberry and loganberry canes. Sometimes, but not often, we were allowed to pick from them and eat, and I preferred the winy flavour of the large loganberries. Beyond the kitchen-garden, on the right, was the entrance to the school quad, and on the left were the stables, which in those days contained no car, not even a horse, only one donkey called Miranda (she was employed in taking the washing to the laundry), and the cottage of the gardener, Charge. Beyond this cottage and behind yet another wall my father had built the School House sanatorium, and near there, in a second kitchen-garden, we children were given small allotments of our own to tend—perhaps six feet square. (I can only remember growing radishes.) My only other gardening activity was to collect snails in a bucket and pour salt on them, so that they exploded into foam. (I was paid so much a hundred for their corpses.) I think I was rather older when I was paid a penny a dozen for killing cabbage-white butterflies with a tennis-racket. This seemed to me a very fine

[44]

sport, and I can sympathize with the interest the Chinese feel when encouraged to kill flies at sight.*

The School House stood in the street called Castle Street which ran down to the canal. On the opposite side were rather inferior shops, not up to the High Street standard: a sweet-shop (one had to climb steps to enter it) where we bought the mineral waters for our manoeuvres; a jeweller's called Bailey's (an old man with a white beard sat perpetually behind the window with a magnifying glass in his eye mending watches and when they read to me about Moses and the Tablets of the Law, I always thought of him); a stationer's and a pawnbroker's where I once tried to pawn a broken cricket-bat but the broker wouldn't accept it.

I had splintered the bat in a clandestine game, beating in bushes near the canal for a lost ball, and I didn't want anyone at home to see the condition it was in. At some stage between eight and ten I had made friends with two or three town boys of what was called then the working-class, and one summer I used to meet them in secret near some rubbish dumps beside the canal. I would bring a bat and a cricket-ball, neither of which they possessed. (Cricket, even in the preparatory school, was still a game: it only became a sport and therefore feared in the senior school.)

This is one of a few memories which remain to me

* I noticed with pleasure one year when I was travelling in the restaurant-car between Hankow and Pekin that there was a fly-swatter beside every place, but alas! there were no flies left to swat. I remember a glorious day in Freetown in 1942 when I closed the windows of my little office and slaughtered more than three hundred flies in a timed four minutes.

[45]

suggesting some social conditioning. Why otherwise should the meetings have remained secret? There were others. During the 1914 war an old woman lived in Castle Street who prepared tripe, and I was given the idea that this was a far lower occupation than a butcher's—it was 'untouchable', though we frequently ate her tripe with white onion sauce. My mother was deeply offended because the tripe-seller's daughter married an officer in the Inns of Court O.T.C., which was stationed for a while in the town (the Corps was regarded by the citizens with some pride because it was not an ordinary regiment—every man was a potential officer as well as a potential barrister).

In the Junior School, which I entered about ten, I became aware too of the stigma attached to those who were 'train boys'. A day-boy was as respectable as a boarder, but a train-boy was not. (Claud Cockburn, who lived at Tring only a few miles away, avoided the stigma because he was sent as a boarder to my father's School House.) The idea was fostered by many of the masters. Train-boys were re-garded as dirty (no wonder, after half an hour on the L.N.W.R. burning war-time fuel), and the fact that many were aided by L.C.C. grants was held against them too. At a later date my father, who unlike my mother was quite with-out social prejudice, tried to remove the stigma by giving them a house and a housemaster and calling them Adders, but it was not a very helpful choice of name. It needed moral courage to be friends with a 'train bug', as they were called, but I can't remember any feeling stronger than a certain illicit toleration which I felt towards the dirtiest of the lot.

He was once caned in public in my form room by my father for some offence which was never made clear to any of us, but we were accustomed at that age to the moral confusion of adults and we didn't trouble to ask him the reason.

Though my father was completely free from social snobbery I noticed a certain exaggerated interest in royalty which was exhibited by my mother and by the aunts who were temporarily in-waiting around her, and I was obscurely irritated; it seemed to lower our family pride, though I was ready enough to accept the glamour of royalty in fiction, in the imaginary world of Ruritania and Kravonia.

I slept at first in the same room as Hugh, who for a long period, it seems to me now, made me pass hours of sleeplessness with his crying. When I went to bed, I had to creep by a kind of branch line on the main staircase that ran steeply up to my mother's private lavatory, which lay in a tower over the terrace at one end of the school quad. My father never used this lavatory, I think, but the children sometimes did, and at night this narrow climbing stair on the way to bed was the point of terror: anything might lurk there in ambush.

I shared my bed with a multitude of soft animals of which I can remember a teddy bear (the most loved), a glove bear (it came second in my affection because it could not stand alone), and a blue plush bird (it was the age of Maeterlinck). I kept the bird, I think, only for the sake of filling the bed, because I disliked the feel of plush and I have mentioned my terror of birds. When quiet had fallen on the house, the fear of fire would emerge like smoke and I would imagine I had been deserted by all my family. I would drop the teddy bear out of bed and shout for the nurse or nursery-maid to pick it up. When one of them came, I felt assured again that all was normal, and I could sleep, though once I remember getting out of bed and sitting on the top of the stairs in order that I might hear the voices from the dining-room below, the low comforting drone of dull adult conversation which told me that the house was not yet ablaze.

My favourite toys in those days were a clockwork train and lead soldiers. When the soldiers had lost too many limbs to stand up we melted them down in a frying-pan over the nursery fire and dropped them into cold water as people do now in Sweden on New Year's night, seeking omens of the future. (I remember well the unmistakable question mark I fished out of the water one Stockholm night which fixed in lead my doubt of the future.) When I was a bit older (about twelve) I would play with Hugh, who was six, an elaborate war game based on H. G. Wells's book *Little Wars*. In the holidays we were able to use the big tables in the School House dining-hall. We would push two tables together and lay out a whole countryside. There were roads marked in chalk and cottages and forests of twigs and rivers which had to be crossed. One game might last a week, with perhaps two hundred men on either side, quick raids by cavalry and slow advances by infantry, measured on lengths of string, mêlées which led to the capture of prisoners, and bombardments with the two 4·2 naval guns. It was 1916, but war was still glamorous to a child.

I passed too through a Meccano period, adding box to box each Christmas, but I had little skill as an engineer. For hobbies (a hobby is an almost compulsive necessity of childhood) I collected stamps. I sold my collection later to Hugh for cash which he always seemed to have easily available— he must have hoarded his weekly twopences, though I never discovered where, and bought with the proceeds books on Antarctic exploration. (The Arctic never interested me because it was all sea.) I day-dreamed of being taken on an expedition as a sea-scout, and when I was about ten I wrote to Doctor Bruce, the explorer, and criticized several statements in his book on Polar Exploration in the Home University Library. I received a courteous and defensive reply.

I collected cigarette cards too, and for a very brief period, because somebody gave me a special album for them, postmarks, but I found these rather abstract and there was no Stanley Gibbons catalogue to indicate whether Penang was more valuable than Angmering. Crests and postcards too had their appropriate albums, and I remember another toy, a monorail car. I have never seen one since. The thin steel single rails were tricky to fasten and the car never kept to them long, swaying wildly, losing balance and plunging to earth. I should be nervous today of travelling by monorail.

The books on the nursery shelves which interested me most were *The Little Duke* by Charlotte M. Yonge (the memory of this book returned to me when I was writing *The Ministry of Fear* and when I revised the novel after the war I inserted chapter headings from *The Little Duke*), *The*

Children of the New Forest by Captain Marryat, the Andrew Lang Fairy Books, the E. Nesbits, of which I liked best *The Enchanted Castle, The Phoenix and the Carpet, Five Children and It* (the less fantastic *The Would-Be-Goods* and *The Treasure Seekers* never meant much to me). Two incidents from these books have always remained vivid to me, one of terror and one of joyful excitement: the Ugly Wugglies made of masks and umbrellas in *The Enchanted Castle* who suddenly came alive and applauded the children's play from their roofless mouths, clapping empty gloves, and the end of *The Phoenix*, when the magical bird has gone and a great box arrives full of everything the children have ever desired: 'toys and games and books, and chocolate and candied cherries, and paint-boxes and photographic cameras'—Brownies they would have been in those days. I think I read alone, but perhaps it was read aloud to us, Kipling's *Baa Baa Black Sheep*, which was like a warning not to take happiness in childhood for granted. At an earlier period of course there was Beatrix Potter. I have never lost my admiration for her books and I have often reread her, so that I am not surprised when I find in one of my own stories, *Under the Garden*, a pale echo of Tom Kitten being trounced up by the rats behind the skirting-board and the sinister Anna-Maria covering him with dough, and in *Brighton Rock* the dishonest lawyer, Prewitt, hungrily echoes Miss Potter's dialogue as he watches the secretaries go by carrying their little typewriters.

Towards the end of this period in my life I came on Henty. We had on the nursery shelves a long run of Henty, and I particularly liked the dull historical parts. 'The XIVth Hussars proceeded in close order to the top of the ridge. On the right flank were the Second Ghurkas...' Rider Haggard I discovered after Henty. My favourite, of course, was *King Solomon's Mines*, but the later adventures of Quatermain bored me. I fell fast in love with Nada the Lily, and because of his savagery I admired Chaka, the great King of Zululand. Later I read *The Brethren* (about the crusades), from which a great phrase remains in my mind to this day, 'So they went, talking earnestly of all things, but, save in God, finding no hope at all', *The Wanderer's Necklace* (a romance of Byzantium in which the hero is blinded by the woman he loves), and *Ayesha*, the sequel to *She*. I didn't at all care for romantic *She*, and found the metaphysical love story sloppy as I find it today (I have always preferred Freud to Jung). But the scene in *Ayesha* when the mad Khan goes hunting with bloodhounds the lord who had courted his wife held me with the strange attraction of suffering and cruelty. 'What followed I will not describe, but never shall I forget the scene of those two heaps of worrying wolves, and of the maniac Khan, who yelled in his fiendish joy, and cheered on his death-hounds to finish their red work.' *Montezuma's Daughter* led me to read and reread a history of Mexico in the school library; the dark night of Cortez' retreat from Mexico City along the narrow causeways haunts me still. What a happy chance it seemed in those days to be the son of the headmaster, for in the holidays all the shelves of the library were open to me, with thousands of books only waiting to be explored.

To Stanley Weyman I must have been introduced fairly early, because I seem to remember my favourite, *The Story of Francis Cludde* (a story of the persecution of Protestants in Queen Mary's reign) being read aloud to me, but it may have been during one of my periodic illnesses. (These agreeably broke up the endless years of childhood: two attacks of measles, a threatened mastoid, jaundice, pleurisy.) There were other Stanley Weymans which were nearly as important to me: *Count Hannibal* (with the masochism of the scorned lover who finally conquers the proud beauty) and *The Abbess of Vlaye*, which perhaps I valued because I had stolen it with some risk from the local W. H. Smith's store. Other books which I have since bought and reread for old time's sake are *The Lost Column*, a story of the Boxer Rebellion, and *The Pirate Aeroplane*, both by Captain Gilson. *The Pirate Aeroplane* made a specially deep impression with its amiable American villain. One episode, when the young hero who is to be shot at dawn for trying to sabotage the pirate plane, plays rummy with his merciless and benevolent captor was much in my mind when I wrote about a poker game in *England Made Me*. I bought *Chums* every week and I remember in particular a fine pirate serial which rivalled *Treasure Island*—by what forgotten author? —and a fascinating account of a world war which began with a coolie strike in the Port of London. (I would force my brother Hugh to lie quiet on the sofa for hours while I read it to him.)

The influence of early books is profound. So much of the future lies on the shelves: early reading has more influence on conduct than any religious teaching. I feel certain that I would not have made a false start, when I was twenty-one, in the British American Tobacco Company, which had promised me a post in China, if I had never read Captain Gilson's *Lost Column*, and without a knowledge of Rider Haggard would I have been drawn later to Liberia? (This led to a wartime post in Sierra Leone. At Oxford I had made tentative enquiries about the Nigerian Navy as a future career.) And surely it must have been *Montezuma's Daughter* and the story of the disastrous night of Cortez' retreat which lured me twenty years afterwards to Mexico. *The Man-eaters of Tsavo* on the other hand fixed in me a boring image of East Africa which even Hemingway was powerless to change. Only an assignment to report the Mau-Mau rebellion in 1951 and the sense of continuous danger on the Kikuyu roads was able to remove it.

Poetry at this period meant very little to me. There were many fatuous verses in the anthology we were given in the prep school, like Allingham's 'Up the Airy Mountain' and Tennyson's 'The Brook'. On one occasion we were told to learn any poem we chose by heart, and I got a certain undeserved credit for learning a long ballad about the brave Lord Willoughby, but it was the only poem in the anthology that I found of any interest. 'Horatius' had too many classical allusions, and I was too young to appreciate 'After Blenheim'. 'Barbara Frietchie' was better, but 'Lord Ullin's Daughter' was awful, so awful that it has crept into several of my stories, an inescapable symbol of fatuity.

[53]

My severe attitude towards 'Horatius' all the same must have been adopted later at school, for I have come across a questionnaire which I answered when I was seven years old in the *School House Gazette*. (Apparently I received the second prize for my 'confessions'—twelve tubes of water-colours.)

What is your greatest aim in life? To go up in an aeroplane.
What is your idea of happiness? Going up to London.
Who is the greatest living statesman? Don't know any.
Who is your favourite character in fiction? Dixon Brett.
What are the qualities you most admire in men? Good looks.
In women? Cleanliness.
What is your favourite pastime? Playing Red Indians.
What is your pet hobby? Collecting coins.
What is your favourite quotation? 'I with two more to help
   me will hold the foe in play.'
Who is the author you like best and which book? Scott. *The
   Talisman.*
Who is the cricketer you most admire? Herbert Greene.
Which is your favourite holiday resort? Overstrand.

Aeroplanes. I have mentioned our failure to see Blériot on the London to Manchester flight, so that perhaps the first aeroplane I actually saw was one I watched through the nursery window above the school playing-fields. Suddenly it nose-dived. I heard later that the pilot was an old boy of the school (his name I think was Wimbush). His younger brother was on the playing-fields, he knew his brother was

[54]

in the plane, and he saw it crash. He walked quickly away down the hill to the school, saying nothing. Often since then watching planes cross the sky, I half-expect to see them fall to earth, as though it were my gaze which had caused that first crash.

Once an airship, captained by an old boy, came down in the grounds of Berkhamsted Castle and remained there for some days on show. The stationer even made picture post-cards of it. It was long before I saw another airship, though I can remember being woken and wrapped in blankets and brought to a bathroom window to see a blaze in the night sky from a Zeppelin which had been shot down over Potters Bar.

Being in London. Once a year we were all taken to *Peter Pan.* I loved it wholeheartedly. My favourite scene was the one where Peter Pan fought alone against the pirates with his sword, and narrowly second to it was the moment of enjoyable horror when the green-lit face of Captain Hook appeared at a service hatch and put poison in Peter's glass. The dying Tinker Bell touched me, but never would I con-sent to call out with the audience that I believed in fairies. It would have been dishonest, for I had never believed in them, except for the period of the play. There was one scene with attractive mermaids which to my great disappointment was cut, for reasons, I think, of war-time economy, from later productions. I could have dispensed more easily with the house in the tree-tops, for I never cared for Wendy, but 'To die will be an awfully big adventure' was a line which echoed through all my adolescence; it only really faded from

[55]

my mind when death became for all of us a common every-day risk. At a later age, when I was twelve, I was taken to a revival of *The Admirable Crichton*. The heroine, Lady Some-body or other, who dressed in animal skins on the desert island, disturbed me for many nights, and she is one of my earliest sexual memories. Was it Cathleen Nesbitt who played the part? If so, those disturbed nights had been experienced not long before by Rupert Brooke, but it was not 'mother comfort' I sought even at that age. It was some years before I was again so sexually moved by a play, and then it was at *Christopher Sly*. The beautiful actress who played with Matheson Lang and was his wife wore a long white silk nightdress which proved just as exciting as the animal skins.

When we went to London we usually had lunch with a retired colonel of the Indian Army called Henry Wright and his wife, our great-aunt Maud, at 11, Belgrave Road—always known to me as Number 11. Maud had introduced Robert Louis Stevenson to his first great love, Mrs Sitwell, who was tied to an unwanted alcoholic husband, but that, of course, meant nothing to me then. It was the vast chamber-pot produced after lunch from the side-board cupboard by Colonel Wright, a relic of Victorian manners, which im-pressed me. He was my godfather, a bluff man, bearded like Edward VII, who walked with the help of sticks because of gout, I suspect, though he claimed to my brother Raymond that he had a cork leg. Before we left for the theatre he held out a hand to each of us concealing a half-crown piece. He died during the First World War and left me a gold watch. My mother sold it for five pounds and put the money for me into war-savings; for more than a quarter of a century afterwards this was my only inheritance.

In later years, after Colonel Wright's death, we were always taken to the Florence Restaurant in Soho, where to my constant surprise a black man in Oriental costume brought the coffee. I wasn't allowed coffee and I was always afraid we would not get to the theatre before the curtain rose. Grown-ups seemed slow at eating and drinking and too blasé about the theatre to be safe companions, particularly my uncle Graham if he happened to make one of the party. I had the unhappy impression that he had come to see his family and not the play.

Qualities most admired in men. My favourite and youngest uncle, Frank, the only uncle on my mother's side of the Greenes, was tall and good-looking and intellectual. I used to see very little of him at this time except at Christmas which he spent with us. I felt shy of him. He understood me too well, and though I liked him, he was a danger to my privacy. He was a civil servant in the Board of Education and he married the daughter of Doctor Todhunter, the Irish poet, when I was about seven. He was the most literary-minded of all my uncles and aunts and he liked walking. When I was older, he, Raymond and I would go on foot to Boxing-day meets of a local pack, and to this day, as I write, I can feel the hard rungs of the furrows under the feet, see the fumes of the riders' breath, and hear the horns and the shouts sharp as ice. Until the hounds moved off we were never certain that the hunt would not be cancelled and we would lose the cry when the fox was sighted and the dabs of scarlet racing over the winter fields. Frank died in the late 1920s from appendicitis, and except for my cousin St George Lake, killed in France, he was the first relative I had to mourn.

Favourite quality in women. I think my reply to this question was probably motivated by disdain, for I find in the *School House Gazette*, from a Table Talk written by my aunt, that I had a good deal of undeserved contempt for my elder sister Molly and through her for girls in general—a contempt which I was soon to lose. My interjections were pointed and repetitious: 'You are silly, Molly. Girls are so silly.' 'Girls wouldn't know. They know nuffin.' 'Girls are always slow and always last.'

Favourite pastime. I am mystified by my choice, for I can't remember that I ever played at Red Indians, *The Last of the Mohicans* I find to this day unreadable, and it was before the days of Western films. I have a vague memory of a small bow and arrows with a green velvet handhold with which for a time I shot erratically at a target hung on the apple trees. But I was too bad a shot to continue long.

Pet hobby. The coins were any foreign coins which came my way and they were piled together in a box which later contained other treasures: a replica of the *Lusitania* medal said to have been given by the German authorities to the crew of the submarine which sank her and a postcard from the Western front, written to me by my red-haired cousin St George—a form with such printed information as 'I am well', 'I am in hospital', with the inapplicable phrases struck out. He provided me too with a spiked Uhlan helmet containing a convincing bloodstain. I wept a long time at the news that he had been killed, and perhaps I have never again felt a death so keenly. In childhood eternity has no meaning —a child has not learnt to hope.

Favourite quotation. This reply surprises me, for I remember liking better Aytoun's 'The Execution of Montrose', which combined heroism and injustice. A child learns about injustice early.

Favourite author. Scott and Dickens were available to me in an admirable series of square books published by Blackie, the Told to the Children series, with coloured illustrations. *Oliver Twist* was in this series and *Peveril of the Peak*. The original text was preserved as far as possible, but dull descriptive passages were blue-pencilled.

Cricket. My eldest brother was the only cricketer I knew, so my praise was not exaggerated. I remember how at Overstrand I went with him to a county match, and he asked me to collect the autographs of the team, who he thought would be more amenable to the request of a little boy. The captain used my head as a desk to write on, and I experienced much more spiritual elevation than I felt at fourteen from the hand of a bishop at confirmation. Only once, on a later occasion, did I collect a signature, when I ran, in my school cap, after G. K. Chesterton, as he laboured like a Lepanto galleon down Shaftesbury Avenue.

Favourite holiday resort. Littlehampton, where we went at Easter, was thought by my mother to be a vulgar resort in the summer, visited by the wrong people, so that we used to go to Overstrand in Norfolk instead. On the cliffs above lay

Poppyland, scarlet fields of poppies known as the Garden of Sleep, and I have always imagined Swinburne's 'Deserted Garden' to have lain somewhere there. Littlehampton meant more to me, and I remember it better: the goat carriages on the green (I was photographed in one at my ambiguous curly age); the beach of silver sand where sea anemones could be found, which had to be reached by ferry, a foreign place, like the garden across the road, not to be visited every day; picnics in Arundel Park to which we set off by carriage to the sound of clopping hoofs (so that later I loved Alfred Noyes's poem, 'The highwayman came riding, up to the old inn-door').*

The elder children took riding lessons from a Miss Reeves and her groom Keenie, a meagre sour creature, whom nobody liked; even his name was ignoble. I started lessons when I was about eight, and I enjoyed them well enough, but fear mingled with the pleasure. The first time I was off the leading rein, as I approached the big iron bridge that spanned the Arun, my pony took fright and jumped a ditch and a hedge. I gained great credit because I kept in my saddle after the jump and fell off only after a discreet interval, the first of many credits I have received for failing.

2

The school began just beyond my father's study, through a

* I plead guilty to ingratitude. Thirty years later Noyes threatened me with an action for libel when I wrote a review of his autobiography.

green baize door. The passage led to the old hall where we were able to play in the holidays, another to the matron's room and the terrace. One matron, Miss Wills, embarrassed me on my seventh birthday by kissing me when I brought her a piece of my birthday cake, so that I returned to the family circle, angry and shattered by the experience. My aunt Nono wrote some verses on the subject in the *School House Gazette*—'Miss Wills kissed me when we met, As I took my birthday cake in . . .' and I had the uncomfortable sense that now the incident would never be forgotten: it had been immortalized by art.

You could get to the school also by going past the dark room and linen-cupboard on the nursery landing, through a glass door, to the dormitories. As I had the freedom of these regions only out of term, they are always empty in my memory—stony, ugly, deserted.

I went to school just before I was eight, as my birthday came in October, after term had started. My form master in the bottom form was called Frost. Later the school was re-organized and he was put in charge of the preparatory school which occupied a house in which my aunt Maud had once lived—it was there that I first read *Dracula* with great fear one long summer afternoon. The memory is salt with the taste of blood, for I had picked my lip while reading and it wouldn't stop bleeding—I thought I was going to bleed to death, one of Count Dracula's victims.

Frost had the reputation of getting on well with very small boys, but I was a little afraid of him. He used to sweep his black gown around him in a melodramatic gesture, before he indulged his jovial ogrish habit of screwing a fist in one's cheek till it hurt.

Of my first day at school I can remember nothing except that I had to read a passage from *Captain Cook's Voyages*, the set English book that term. I found the formal eighteenth-century prose very dull, and I still do. History was my favourite subject, and when I was about twelve a rather foolish master whom we all despised stated in my annual report, otherwise given up to laconic statements— 'Satisfactory', 'Tries hard', 'weak' and suchlike—that I 'had the makings of an historian'. I was pleased, but considered rightly that it was an attempt to pander favour with my father.

At this period I was not unhappy at school except that, when I was twelve and I was moved into the top junior form, I remained at the bottom of the class for a whole term and lost my confidence. Of the masters I remember a monstrously fat one called Moir with black hair which was thinly streaked across the top of a bald head. Poor man, he must have suffered from some glandular disease which rendered him unfit for military service. He married during the war to everyone's astonishment a pretty young woman who was a temporary mistress; it seemed the mating of Beauty and the Beast. A popular master in charge of one of the junior houses was called Simpson. He was never properly shaved, the five o'clock shadow was there at morning prayers, and he had four chins, although he was not otherwise a fat man. He rubbed his hands together in a gloating manner when in form he caught one who belonged to his house in a punishable offence. He would refer jocularly to beatings and he very obviously enjoyed them. In a strange way this made him popular. It seemed to me even then that his boys were collaborators in a pleasure.

I can remember nothing about games, except that once I teased my cousin Tooter, who ran home from the playing-fields, crying. I felt a great shame at this, I knew already in my heart that I belonged on the side of the victims, not of the torturers, and this was a betrayal of all those sunlit after-noons on the roof of the Hall. These were the old playing-fields near the railway station, beyond Berkhamsted Castle, and when war came they were taken over by what was called Kitchener's Army and to this day they are known as Kitchener's Fields. (My rich uncle came to the rescue of the school and lent the governors enough money to buy far better fields at the top of the hill where my sister's pug was killed.)

The only class I actively hated was held in the gym. I was very bad at gymnastics and all life long my instinct has been to abandon anything for which I have no talent; tennis, golf, dancing, sailing, all have been abandoned, and perhaps it is only desperation which keeps me writing, like someone who clings to an unhappy marriage for fear of solitude. I parti-cularly disliked trying to vault or to climb a rope. I suffered in those days, like a character of mine, Jones, in *The Comedians*, from flat feet, and I had to wear supports inside my shoes and have massage from a gym mistress. The massage tickled a little and my soles sometimes ached, but on the whole I found the treatment agreeable, perhaps be-

cause it was given by a woman. This must have been between the age of ten and twelve, for it was the war of 1914
which brought a number of mistresses to the school in place
of the masters who had joined the army.

The memory of August 1914 is associated with my uncle's
house at Harston. The lawn in front of the house had a high
wall. One could see over it only by climbing the chunky
roots of old trees covered in ivy and swarming with spiders.
Troops were continually passing through in these first days
and they rested on the village green; once I was sent out
with a basket of apples to refresh them. Herbert bicycled in
from Cambridge one day with the evening paper announcing
the fall of Namur. My brothers and I were delighted at the
speed with which it had fallen because the prolonged defence of Liège had threatened a speedy termination of the
war. As long as the war continued, we might one day be
involved, and the world of Henty seemed to come a little
nearer. Perhaps there would be an invasion, as in William
Le Queux's famous documentary novel, and Berkhamsted
Common, I believed, would be ideal for the exploits of one
young *franc-tireur*. Indeed there were dramatic incidents
even in Berkhamsted. A German master was denounced to
my father as a spy because he had been seen under the railway bridge without a hat, a dachshund was stoned in the
High Street, and once my uncle Eppy was summoned at
night to the police station and asked to lend his motor-car to
help block the Great North Road down which a German
armoured car was said to be advancing towards London. A
colonel of the Inns of Court O.T.C. was also at the station.

[64]

'Five hundred rifles,' he lamented, 'and not a round of live ammunition.' My uncle was sceptical, but he lent his car.

But the war ended too soon for us, and only Herbert became lightly involved, when he was promoted lance-corporal in the H.A.C. He never reached France and one day he returned home without his single stripe. It was only a long time afterwards that I learned the reason—a sympathetic one. He was in charge of a spy who was awaiting execution in the Tower (he added the spy's autograph to his collection), and on the occasion of an air-raid he let the prisoner out of his cell to share the fun. Otherwise we were touched closely only twice—by the death of St George and by the disappearance of our new nurse's fiancé—'missing, believed killed'. She was a kind dumpy young woman called Olive Dodge with an agreeable face like a penny bun with two currants for eyes (the most you could expect in war-time), and we were sad for her, knowing as our parents told us that there was little or no hope. Yet she never lost her hope and one day the miracle happened—he was discovered in a London hospital with shell-shock. He didn't recognize her, he was plunged in deep melancholia, but she never despaired, and one day she was able proudly to introduce him to the denizens of the nursery, a very tall dark man with a small moustache who spoke hardly at all. They married and lived happily ever after, or so I hope, in Acton.

At some point that year I abandoned the effort of trying to vault or climb a rope or scramble on the parallel bars, and I pretended, whenever that class came round, that I was ill. I would walk up on to the Common and stay there, hidden among the gorse bushes with their yellow flowers until school was over. Once lying flat in the bracken by the side of the road I saw the gardener Charge go by with the family donkey-cart. My parents, when I told them years later, denied that this was possible, because they said he could have had no business up there far away from the laundry and the town, but how could I have imagined Miranda? Perhaps he was out for his own personal pleasure on a sunny June day. I enjoyed the feeling of being safely hidden among the bushes while he went by, even if I were not yet hunted. The long secret trek through the heather by Alan Breck and David Balfour always for me took place on Berkhamsted Common; it almost seemed a personal adventure, perhaps because my mother was kin to the Balfours of Pilrig, and indeed first cousin to Stevenson himself.

I don't know how long these sporadic escapes went on. They turned at some point (I would guess when I was eleven) into a better organized and a more prolonged truancy. By this time I was having breakfast in the dining-room with my elders, and not in the nursery with five-year-old Hugh and the baby Elisabeth. At the end of breakfast I would gather up my school-books as though going across to prayers.

I should explain that the school day began with prayers of a rather lay variety—masters on a platform, boys below—in what was called Deans' Hall which was named after Dean Incent, the sixteenth-century founder of Berkhamsted School, but also—the position of the apostrophe was important—after Doctor Fry, my father's sinister sadistic pre-

[66]

decessor and kinsman by marriage, who had become the Dean of Lincoln.

This Manichaean figure in black gaiters with a long white St Peter's beard sometimes came to stay. After breakfast on these occasions it was my mother's duty to clear the hall outside the dining-room of maids and children, so that the Dean could go to the lavatory unobserved and emerge again unseen by anyone. As a headmaster he had been known as a flogger, and he thus made a life-long enemy of one old Berkhamstedian, later my Oxford tutor, Kenneth Bell, who one day had his cap snatched off by a school bully and was then beaten by Fry who saw him in the street without it. Fry as Dean of Lincoln became a popular lecturer in the United States where he went at regular intervals to procure money for restoring Lincoln Cathedral. On his last voyage, as he returned first-class in a Cunarder, fate overtook him and showed him up as the absurd figure he had always been. He had suffered a stroke before embarking which damaged his powers of speech and his neighbours at table overheard him asking his son Charley, the Vicar of Maidenhead, for certain shocking objects when all he had in mind was a soft-boiled egg. Charley, who for years vainly paid court to my beautiful aunt Nono, was a far more likeable figure. He was so fat that he looked like a black tennis-ball, and to amuse us he would put two chairs together and bounce over them— not jump. 'Bounce for us, Cousin Charley, bounce for us,' we would cry, while my aunt watched with cynical disdain. She couldn't respect a man who bounced.

Instead of going to Deans' Hall I would wait in the garden

[67]

until I knew the school was safely assembled, for fear that I might meet other boys or masters, and then I would walk up the High Street. My purpose was to steal something to read from the local W. H. Smith's store. I can only remember two occasions, but I think there must have been others: once I stole a copy of *The Railway Magazine* and once, as I have mentioned, *The Abbess of Vlaye* by Stanley Weyman, a sixpenny paperback with double columns. My reading matter thus obtained, I would return home. This must have been an even trickier matter than the theft as I had to go by the windows of the dining-room where the maid would be clearing breakfast, but I suppose at the height I had reached then it was quite easy to stoop below their level. That danger safely past I would go cautiously out to the croquet lawn, past the buddleia and the butterflies, and swing the summer-house round so that it faced a flower-bed and the sanatorium wall; there I sat comfortably in a deck-chair and read my stolen book until the school broke up for lunch. I followed the same routine, without the foray to the High Street, in the afternoon, and recklessly I carried my truancy on until the last day of term. I was in the form of a Mr Davis and my father, who was making a rapid tour of the classrooms on the last day, was asked by Davis how my illness was progressing. It must have been quite a shock for my father who knew of no illness in his family. He came back home and out to the shelter where I was discovered ... or rather I think he sent my mother. (Perhaps the search was proceeding in many directions at once.) I was told to go to bed, and when I was in my nightshirt my father came up and caned me.

This is the only beating I can remember, but at school I would invent apocryphal stories of having been cruelly flogged—it gave me the status which a headmaster's son lacked. I was in the middle of some story of brutal cruelty during a break between classes in the quad when a 'scrumming' took place. This was a strange kind of lemming drive which at intervals afflicted the lower school. A rumour would start that an extra half-holiday was going to be given (which happened fairly frequently during the war, whenever an old boy had been decorated with a D.S.O. or an M.C. A V.C. ranked as a whole holiday, but this only happened twice.) The rumours, however often they proved to be wrong, caused the whole junior school to press up against the terrace during a break and stay crammed there until my father would appear and send us packing. Occasionally the rumour proved true and so confirmed the idea that we had actually caused the half-holiday by our scrumming.

Magic and incantation play a great part in childhood. There was a tuckshop by the fives-court which was only open, because of war-shortages, to boys of the senior school. As a junior I would stand outside reciting an accepted formula, 'Treat I', to any older boy as he came out, and occasionally one would detach a morsel of bun and hand it over. The favourite purchase was a penny currant bun with a bar of chocolate inside, though it was seldom that any chocolate was included in the exiguous treat. I suppose we were always a little hungry in the war years. There were no potatoes and little sugar and we grew deadly tired of substitutes—rice and honey-sugar. My sister Elisabeth, who

[69]

was around two at the time, would have hardly eaten anything at all during our nursery meals if I had not named each spoonful after a war-leader, though what their names could possibly have conveyed to her I cannot imagine. 'This is General Joffre,' I would say, popping in a dreary spoonful of suet, 'and this is General French . . . Hindenburg . . . Allenby.'

The clouds of unknowing were still luminous with happiness. There was no loneliness to be experienced, however occupied the parents might be, in a family of six children, a nanny, a nursemaid, a gardener, a fat and cheerful cook, a beloved head-housemaid, a platoon of assistant maids, a whole battalion of aunts and uncles, all of them called Greene, which seemed to bring them closer, and invariably at Christmas that old bachelor friend who in those days formed part of any large family gathering, a little mocked in secret by the parents, a little resented in secret by the children. The six birthdays, the Christmas play, the Easter and the summer seaside, all arrived like planets in their due season, unaffected by war. Only in the clouds ahead I could see that there was no luminosity at all. Yet anything, I felt, anything, even a romantic death, might happen to save me before my thirteenth year struck.

Chapter 3

I

I had passed thirteen and things were worse even than I had foreseen. I lay in bed in the dormitory of St John's, listening to the footsteps clatter down the stone stairs to early prep. and breakfast, and when the silence had safely returned I began trying to cut my right leg open with a penknife. But the knife was blunt and my nerve was too weak for the work.

I was back in the house of my early childhood, but the circumstances had changed. The garden across the road, France across the Channel, was now closed to me: I could no longer set foot in the chintzy drawing-room where my mother had read aloud to us and where I had wept over the story of the children buried by the birds. In those early days I had not even been aware that there existed in the same house such grim rooms as those I lived in now. Even the door by which I entered the house was a different one, a side door like a service entrance, though no servant would have endured the squalor we lived in.* There was a schoolroom

---

* Memory often exaggerates, but some twelve years ago, because I had started a novel about a school, I revisited the scene and found no change. I abandoned the novel—I couldn't bear mentally living again for several years in these surroundings. A leper colony in the Congo was preferable, so I went to Yonda in search of a burnt-out case.

with ink-stained nibbled desks insufficiently warmed by one cast-iron stove, a changing-room smelling of sweat and stale clothes, stone stairs, worn by generations of feet, leading to a dormitory divided by pitch-pine partitions that gave inadequate privacy—no moment of the night was free from noise, a cough, a snore, a fart. Years later when I read the sermon on hell in Joyce's *Portrait of the Artist* I recognized the land I had inhabited. I had left civilization behind and entered a savage country of strange customs and inexplicable cruelties: a country in which I was a foreigner and a suspect, quite literally a hunted creature, known to have dubious associates. Was my father not the headmaster? I was like the son of a quisling in a country under occupation. My elder brother Raymond was a school prefect and head of the house—in other words one of Quisling's collaborators. I was surrounded by the forces of the resistance, and yet I couldn't join them without betraying my father and my brother. My cousin Ben, a junior prefect, one of the rich Greenes, had no such scruples and worked covertly against my brother, gaining much popularity in consequence, so that I felt the less sympathy for him when he was later imprisoned, without warrant or reason, in the second German war under Regulation 18b. Injustice had bred injustice.

Though children can be abominably cruel, no physical tortures were inflicted on me. If I had possessed any skill at games I might even have won a tacit acceptance into the resistance movement, but I hated rugger only one degree less than I now hated cricket—a sport which at six years old

I had loved as a game. 'Runs' I enjoyed, for then I could be alone in the solitude of the countryside, and at this period of my life I loved the country. It was my natural escape-route. On the wide stretches of Berkhamsted Common, seamed with the abandoned trenches of the Inns of Court O.T.C. among the gorse and heather, and in the Ashridge beech-woods beyond, I could dramatize my loneliness and feel I was one of John Buchan's heroes making his hidden way across the Scottish moors with every man's hand against him.

I grew clever at evasion. Truancy was impressed as the pattern of my life. To avoid fielding-practice I invented extra coaching in mathematics after school; I even named the master who I said was teaching me and curiously enough my story was never investigated. I would slip out of St John's with a book in my pocket while others were changing and make my way a little up the hill where a small lane branched off into the countryside. It was one of the most solitary lanes I have ever known; not even courting couples were to be seen there, perhaps because it was hardly wide enough for two to walk abreast. On one side was a ploughed field: on the other a ditch with a thick hawthorn hedge which was hollow in the centre and in which I could sit concealed and read my book. What book? I cannot be sure now. The days of Henty were over—my body was leading my brain in unfamiliar directions. I found extraordinary beauty and passion, I remember, in Sir Lewis Morris's *Epic of Hades*, and perhaps I was reading lines like these spoken by Helen of Troy:

[73]

> Was it love
> That drew me then to Paris? He was fair,
> I grant you, fairer than a summer morn,
> Fair with a woman's fairness, yet in arms
> A hero, but he never had my heart.
> It was not he seduced me, but the thirst
> For freedom, if in more than thought I erred,
> And was not rapt but willing. For my child,
> Born to an unloved father, loved me not,
> The fresh sea called, the galleys plunged, and I
> Fled willing from my prison and the pain
> Of undesired caresses, and the wind
> Was fair, and on the third day as we sailed,
> My heart was glad within me when I saw
> The towers of Ilium rise beyond the wave.

Today the lines seem pinchbeck, and yet they retain the secret smell of my hiding-place.

One comes to literature by devious routes, and it was often Stephen Phillips's *Paolo and Francesca* which I carried with me into hiding, just as another boy may be playing truant now with the verse-plays of Christopher Fry. There *were* lines in that banal drama which faltered on the edge of poetry: 'The last sunset cry of wounded kings', 'the childless cavern cry of the barren sea', and I was not critical in the hawthorn hedge.

The danger of discovery lent those hours a quality of excitement which was very close to momentary happiness. Scent to me is far more evocative than sound or perhaps even sight, so that I become attracted without realizing it to the smell of a floor-polish or a detergent which one day I miss when I open my door and home seems no longer home. So in my sixties I seem able to smell the leaves and grasses of my hiding-place more certainly than I hear the dangerous footsteps on the path or see the countryman's boots pass by on the level of my eyes. I remember how in 1944 I spent a rather guilty night of security in Berkhamsted away from the fly-bombs and the fire-watching with my brother Hugh. Asleep in the Swan Inn I dreamt of the W. H. Smith bookshop down the High Street from which I had stolen *The Railway Magazine* all those years ago, and I smelt the individual smell of the shop which was like the smell of no other Smith's that I have ever known. In my dream I found a book for which I had long been searching on a particular shelf, and so in the morning, before I had breakfast, I walked down the street to see whether my dream might prove true. I was disappointed, the book was not there, but what I noticed at once on entering the shop was that the familiar smell had gone, and without the smell the shop was not the same. I enquired after the manager whom I remembered well: he had died the year before, and I suppose the new manager had changed whatever was the source of the smell which had so long haunted my imagination.

On Sundays we would go for walks, by order, in threes, and the names had to be filled up like a dance programme on a list which was hung up on the changing-room door. This surely must have had some moral object, though one which eludes me today when I remember how deftly the

'Emperor's Crown' used to be performed by three girls at once in a brothel in Batista's Havana. Three can surely be as dangerous company as two, or were the authorities cynical enough to believe that in every three there would be one informer?

The housemaster in my first year was Mr Herbert, an old silver-haired bachelor, whose formidable sister cared for him better than she did the boys. To add to my inextricable confusion of loyalties he happened to be my godfather, mysteriously linked at my birth to look after my spiritual well-being with that formidable gouty Colonel Wright of Number 11, who owned the chamber-pot in the dining-room cupboard. Mr Herbert was certainly not a cynic. He was an innocent little white rabbit of a bachelor, dominated by the dark Constance, his sister; he must have possessed a passion for birds because he later became the private secretary to Lord Grey of Falloden in that statesman's blind retirement. My only memory of him is seated at a desk in the St John's schoolroom on the first evening of my first term there, while each boy in turn submitted to him, for censorship or approval, any books he had brought from home to read. The danger was in the source—home, where dwelt unreliable and uncelibate parents. Anything in the school library was acceptable—even the inflammatory blank verse of Sir Lewis Morris from whom I later learned of the carnal loves of Helen and Cleopatra.

The methods of censorship are always curiously haphazard. In the 1950s I was to be summoned by Cardinal Griffin to Westminster Cathedral and told that my novel

The Power and the Glory, which had been published ten years before, had been condemned by the Holy Office, and Cardinal Pizzardo required changes which I naturally— though I hope politely—refused to make. Cardinal Griffin remarked that he would have preferred it if they had condemned *The End of the Affair*. 'Of course,' he said, 'you and I receive no harm from erotic passages, but the young . . .' I told him, and it was true enough, though I had forgotten the evil influence of Sir Lewis Morris, that one of my earliest erotic experiences had been awoken by *David Copperfield*. Our interview at that point came abruptly to an end, and he gave me, as a parting shot, a copy of a pastoral letter which had been read in the churches of his diocese, condemning my work by implication. (Unfortunately I thought too late of asking him to autograph it.) Later, when Pope Paul told me that among the novels of mine he had read was *The Power and the Glory*, I answered that the book he had read had been condemned by the Holy Office. His attitude was more liberal than that of Cardinal Pizzardo. 'Some parts of all your books will always,' he said, 'offend some Catholics. You should not worry about that': a counsel which I find it easy to take.

School rules, like those of the Roman Curia, are slow to change, however temporary the ruler who inspires them may be. I think the censorship of books from home (which was strictly enforced only, like a customs examination, when one passed the border—parcels from home were exempt) was dropped with Mr Herbert's retirement, but other relics of his government remained—the lavatories without locks,

[77]

where each newcomer, anxious to perform his morning duty, had to call out 'Number off' in order to learn which of the compartments was empty; and that rule for Sunday walks which made certain that no one, under any circumstances, would ever walk dangerously alone.

But I was not a member of the resistance—I was Quisling's son. I had often to go begging that my name might be included in groups who had no desire for my company, until at last, after a term or two of purgatory, I received permission from my parents to spend Sunday afternoons at home. It was a relief for which I paid dearly in my nerves—a kind of *coitus interruptus* with the civilized life of home, for as evening fell I had to rejoin my companions tramping into the school chapel and afterwards climb the hill to St John's, and then at night the stone stairs to the dormitory—where at this moment in my memory I have lamentably failed to saw open my knee.

Unhappiness in a child accumulates because he sees no end to the dark tunnel. The thirteen weeks of a term might just as well be thirteen years. The unexpected never happens. Unhappiness is a daily routine. I imagine that a man condemned to a long prison sentence feels much the same. I cannot remember what particular item in the routine of a boarding-school roused this first act of rebellion—loneliness, the struggle of conflicting loyalties, the sense of continuous grime, of unlocked lavatory doors, the odour of farts (it was sexually a very pure house, there was no hint of homosexuality, but scatology was another matter, and I have disliked the lavatory joke from that age on). Or was it just then

[78]

that I had suffered from what seemed to me a great betrayal? This story at least was to have a satisfactory though remote ending.

2

While I was at St John's I must have read Q's novel *Foe-Farrell* three or four times. It was the dramatic story of a man's revenge, and I very much wanted an opportunity for dramatic revenge. As I remember the tale a political demagogue ruined the experiment of a great surgeon by inciting a mob to wreck his laboratory where it was believed that he was practising vivisection. From that moment the surgeon Foe (or was it Farrell?) pursued Farrell (or was it Foe?) across the world and through the years with the sole object of revenge—I think he even found himself alone in an open boat on the Pacific with his enemy, improbable though this may sound. Then, under the long-drawn torture of the pursuit, the characters changed places: the pursued took on nobility, the pursuer the former vulgarity of his enemy. It was a very moral story, but I don't think it was the moral which interested me—simple revenge was all I wanted.

For there was a boy at my school called Carter who perfected during my fourteenth and fifteenth years a system of mental torture based on my difficult situation. Carter had an adult imagination—he could conceive the conflict of loyalties, loyalties to my age-group, loyalty to my father and brother. The sneering nicknames were inserted like splinters under the nails.

I think in time I might have coped with Carter—there was an element of reluctant admiration, I believe, on both sides. I admired his ruthlessness, and in an odd way he admired what he wounded in me. Between the torturer and the tortured arises a kind of relationship. So long as the torture continues the torturer has failed, and he recognizes an equality in his victim. I never seriously in later years desired revenge on Carter. But Watson was another matter.

Watson was one of my few friends and he deserted me for Carter. He had none of Carter's *finesse*—Carter continually tempted me with offers of friendship snatched away like a sweet, but leaving the impression that somewhere some time the torture would end, while Watson imitated him only at a blundering unimaginative level. Alone he would have had no power to hurt. Nonetheless it was on Watson that I swore revenge, for with his defection my isolation had become almost complete.

For many years after leaving school, when I thought back to that period, I found the desire for revenge alive like a creature under a stone. The only change was that I looked under the stone less and less often. I began to write, and the past lost some of its power—I wrote it out of me. But still every few years a scent, a stretch of wall, a book on a shelf, a name in a newspaper, would remind me to lift the stone and watch the creature move its head towards the light.

In December 1951 I was in the shop of the Cold Storage Company in Kuala Lumpur buying whisky for Christmas which I was going to spend in Malacca. I had just got back from a three-day jungle patrol with the 2/7th Gurkha Rifles in Pahang, seeking communist guerillas, and I was feeling very tired of Malaya. A voice said, 'You are Greene, aren't you?'

A foxy-faced man with a small moustache stood at my elbow.

I said, 'Yes, I'm afraid . . .'

'My name's Watson.'

'Watson?' It must have been a very long time since I had lifted the stone, for the name meant nothing to me at first, nor the flushed colonial face.

'We were at school together, don't you remember? We used to go around with a chap called Carter. The three of us. Why, you used to help me and Carter with our Latin prep.'

At one time, in the days when I still day-dreamed, I would imagine meeting Watson at a cocktail party and in some way humiliating him in public. Nothing could have been more public than the Cold Storage Company of Kuala Lumpur during the Christmas rush, but all I could find to say was, 'I didn't think I was any good at Latin.'

'Better than we were anyway.'

I said, 'What are you doing now?'

'Customs and excise. Do you play polo?'

'No.'

'Come along and see me play one evening.'

'I'm just off to Malacca.'

'When you get back. Talk over old times. What inseparables we were—you and me and old Carter.' It was obvious that his memory held a quite different impression from mine.

'What's happened to Carter?'

'He went into Cables and died.'

I said, 'When I get back from Malacca . . .' and went thoughtfully out.

What an anti-climax the meeting had been. I wondered all the way back to my hotel if I would ever have written a book had it not been for Watson and the dead Carter, if those years of humiliation had not given me an excessive desire to prove that I was good at something, however long the effort might prove. Was that a reason to be grateful to Watson or the reverse? I remembered another ambition—to be a consul in the Levant: I had got so far as sitting successfully for the *viva*. If it had not been for Watson . . . So speculating, I felt Watson sliding out of mind, and when I came back from Malacca I had forgotten him.

Indeed it was only many months later, after I had left Malaya, as I thought, for good, that I remembered I had never rung him up, had never watched him play polo, nor exchanged memories of the three inseparables. Perhaps, unconsciously, that was my revenge—to have forgotten him so easily. Now that I had raised the stone again, I knew that nothing lived beneath it.

3

The last footsteps had receded a long time ago, and I had put away the penknife. If the knife had been less blunt or my nerve had not failed, I wonder how I would have explained the cut knee. But perhaps unconsciously the whole point for me was that the act was inexplicable, like a would-be suicide's uncertain overdose of sleeping pills, something which demands prompt action from outside. Successful suicide is often only a cry for help which hasn't been heard in time.

After a long interval the matron came up to inspect the dormitories and found me in bed. I invented reasons—a feeling of sickness, a headache—which she accepted readily. She was a young woman—though to me then she seemed like all my elders fixed in a kind of static middle-age—who radiated a sense of calm friendliness. The thermometer might accuse me of malingering, but not she. She knew that even a child reaches at a certain moment a psychological limit. I was to stay in bed until after lunch and then take tea in her room. Thus she postponed for another year or more the final act of rebellion. Kindness alas! is often false kindness, enabling one to endure a little longer an almost unbearable situation.

It was on that day that the rain came down in torrents, postponing what I had perhaps stayed in bed to avoid, the weekly parade of the O.T.C. I hated that uniform with the puttees I could never learn to tie with any security or neatness and I dreaded the parades where I always fumbled fixing bayonets or strayed forming fours, under the ironic eyes of Watson and Carter. There was a deadly gravity about these parades because the years of Passchendaele and Galli-poli were only just over; outside the school chapel there was the list of old boys killed, plaque after plaque in double column, to remind us of the recent years. Most of us were shocked when the Eton O.T.C. arrived for a joint field-day with grey uniforms in place of the sacred khaki and with an undisciplined frivolity, which seemed in our over-serious eyes to deny the virtues of the dead.*

The water flowed in torrents down the hill; the gutters overflowed, and now it was a flood which I feared, dams breaking, reservoirs overflowing (I had read about it all in Rider Haggard's *Lysbeth*), but even drowning was prefer-able to the ignoble routine of school. The matron's kindness stood out by its rarity in that world, and perhaps because of its rarity two kind gentle people were drawn together and the assistant housemaster, Mr Dale, whom we had nick-named Dicker, married the matron.

Dicker was a youngish man in those days (though, of course, to me middle-aged) with a bald head and gold-rimmed glasses and a drawl which sometimes became a slight stutter; a difficulty of communication, one would have

* The O.T.C. bred in me a permanent dislike of uniforms. There was a time in 1942 when the authorities at home wished to put me into a naval uniform. I pointed out that to have proper privacy for my secret work I would have to bear the rank of commander. They suggested the Air Force. In that case I must be a group captain, I replied, and then they surrendered. I could call myself C.I.D. Special Branch, they said, and the danger of a uniform was over.

said, and yet to those willing to listen he communicated more than any other master, except perhaps my father. Oddly enough he had no difficulty with discipline, and though he had little obvious popularity, like some of the hearty mud-stained members of the staff, and looked out of place in flapping shorts as he circled the scrum with a whistle in his mouth, no one imitated his drawl, his nickname was innocuous, and the worst joke ever made at his expense was 'Where do the fleas run? Up Hill and down Dale'. Hill, a fine tennis-player and an older man, was Dale's chief friend at the school. Later, when retired, they collaborated in difficult academic crosswords which were published in a Sunday paper under the name of Torquemada. Some of Dale's kindness must have rubbed off on Hill, for I remember how I was once invited to tea by him and how two hours of anchovy-toast and tea-cakes and adult conversation atoned for a week of misery and postponed again the final breakdown. Perhaps it would have been postponed indefinitely if at that period I could have comforted myself with Dale's favourite apophthegm, drawled out in the most distressing circumstances: 'It's all experience.' I remember repeating the phrase to keep my spirits up in April, 1941, as I shambled fearfully down blazing Gower Street in the footsteps of our old Jewish post warden, powerful and imperturbable in his shiny black mackintosh, like a moving statue in malachite, the stone catching the reflection of the flames and flares, one of the bravest men I have known and the most unaware of his own courage.

[85]

4

I think it may have been the interminable repetitions in my life which finally broke me down. A term always lasted thirteen weeks, and contained two 'half-holidays' as they were called, except in summer when there were three. Sundays came every seven days with terrible regularity, like Lazarus with his drop of water; there were no Saints' Days to vary the week, and once a week came the dreaded O.T.C. parade.

I tried out other forms of escape after I failed to cut my leg. Once at home on the eve of term I went into the dark room by the linen-cupboard, and in that red Mephistophelean glare drank a quantity of hypo under the false impression that it was poisonous. On another occasion I drained my blue glass bottle of hay-fever drops, which, as they contained a small quantity of cocaine, were probably good for my despair. A bunch of deadly nightshade, picked and eaten on the Common, had only a slightly narcotic effect, and once, towards the end of one holiday, I swallowed twenty aspirins before swimming in the empty school baths. (I can still remember the curious sensation of swimming through cotton wool.)

I endured that life for some eight terms—a hundred and four weeks of monotony, humiliation and mental pain. It is astonishing how tough a boy can be, but I was helped by my truancies, those peaceful hours hidden in the hedge. At last came the moment of final decision. It was after breakfast one morning in the School House dining-room, on the last day of the summer holidays, that I made my break for liberty. I wrote a note, which I placed on the black oak side-board under the whisky tantalus, saying that instead of re-turning to St John's, I had taken to the Common and would remain there in hiding until my parents agreed that never again should I go back to my prison. There were enough blackberries that fine autumn to keep me from hunger, and I prided myself on knowing every hidden trench. This time it was a quisling who took to the *maquis*. What I cannot re-member arranging was any way by which my parents could communicate the news of their surrender.

There was a wonderful sense of release from all the ten-sion and the indecision as I made my way up the long road lined with Spanish chestnuts from the ruined castle to the slope where the Common began. I had to hurry, for here on this open road I might have been intercepted, but the race against time was part of the excitement on that golden autumn day, with a faint mist lying along the canal, across the watercress beds by the railway viaduct and in the grassy pool of the castle. Then I was safely there, on the Common, among the gorse and bracken of my chosen battlefield.

I had brought a book in my pocket, but I was much too excited to read, for I had a whole campaign to plan. There were two routes a search-party might take, the one by the road I had come and another through Kitchener's Fields which entered the Common by a flank. There was one point of vantage, an abandoned firing-butt, from which I could see anyone who approached for a hundred yards around, but there I would be exposed myself and I didn't like the idea of my rebellion ending in an undignified chase. I wanted to be an invisible watcher, a spy on all that went on, and so I moved restlessly among the bushes on the edge of the Common, watching for the enemy, ready to retreat unseen into the depths, like the *franc-tireurs* of Henty or David Balfour pursued by red-coats or Buchan's Hannay.

It was still too early for the invasion to begin. Immediately after breakfast my mother would be busy with the kitchen, the nursery, the linen-cupboard; my father would be shut in his study working on the Scheme—an elaborate game of his own invention consisting of a large board with slots for vari-coloured cards. With its help he was able to ensure that on the school timetable a master was not allotted contradictory duties, to teach Latin Composition to IV b simultaneously with English literature to V a. Visiting headmasters were introduced to this Scheme with pride, and I think my father took as much pleasure in shifting a pink card to an empty space or solving a difficult problem with a 'free period' in white as in moving a queen to mate at chess or suddenly disrupting an opponent's attack by castling. He would sit over the board for half an hour at a time, motionless, in the attitude of Rodin's Thinker. No one would surely be bold enough to disturb him, while he was bent over his essential game, with my peace-destroying note.

I think at least two hours must have passed, and I would like to know now what conferences were held, what tactics were suggested, what decisions were made. But it is too late for me to find out. All the protagonists are dead except myself—my father, my mother, my elder sister, even the head housemaid who would have known all. I can imagine the bruit extending, in spite of all precautions, upstairs to the nursery and along the passage to the kitchen quarters: what a murmur of under-housemaids and scullery-maids, and the gardener perhaps leaning in at the kitchen-window to catch the latest report. And all this time I had nothing to do but roam my battlefield from bush to bush. My resolution was quite unchanged. I had asserted my freedom. Let others clean up the mess, I was happy, and never in the future—not even when I played Russian roulette on this same Common—did I experience again the hopeless misery of the years which I was escaping now.

It was time I looked at my exposed flank—a steep clay path between oaks and beeches above Kitchener's Fields. I moved rashly out beyond the cover of the bushes and began to descend, until, turning a corner, I came face to face with my elder sister, Molly. I could have run, of course, but that hardly suited the dignity of my protest, and so I went quietly home with her. It was a tactical defeat, but it proved all the same a strategical victory. I *had* changed my life; the whole future was decisively altered.

Perhaps I was nearer a nervous breakdown than I now care to believe, for a thick haze conceals all that happened next. Did I talk to my sister on my tramp home? I think I must have walked in silent pride. How was I greeted? I remember no reproaches, only a well-warmed bed in the spare-room next my parents', which was used only for more serious ailments than the regular family traffic of colds and coughs. I seem to remember my father sitting on the bed and interrogating me seriously and tenderly, and from that interrogation grew a whole comedy of errors. I suppose I complained of the general filth of my life at St John's, meaning the unlocked lavatories, the continual farting of my companions, but he misunderstood me and believed I had been the victim of some ring of masturbation, so that other investigations were now set on foot among the innocent inhabitants of St John's. The truth was I had not yet discovered the pleasure of masturbation and didn't even know the meaning of the word, though my father in any case probably used some vague abstract expression which was equally applicable to breaking wind.

At this date my brother Raymond had started to study medicine at Oxford and he was hastily summoned home for consultation; my father found the situation beyond him—perhaps he even believed the popular fable of his generation that masturbation led to madness, a threat already existing on both sides of the family. His own father, buried in St Kitts, had been a manic-depressive, and my mother's father, an Anglican clergyman, suffered from an exaggerated sense of guilt and, when his bishop refused his request to be defrocked, proceeded to put the matter into effect himself in a field. We were never told anything about that grandparent and I had always assumed he was dead before I was born. Only a few years ago, in reading Swinburne's letters, I learnt from a footnote that he had not died until 1924, so he must have seemed a living menace at this moment in our lives.*

* As an undergraduate at Trinity College, Cambridge, he had been

My brother, who felt great pride at the trust reposed in him (he was only three years older than myself and in his first year at Oxford), suggested psycho-analysis as a possible solution, and my father—an astonishing thing in 1920—agreed.

part-author of a favourable review of the first shocking volume of *Poems and Ballads*. 'Please send me *at once*,' Swinburne wrote to the sinister Hotten in 1867, 'the January number of a Cambridge Magazine called "the Light Blue" containing an article on my Poems.'

Chapter 4

In age I find myself with an interest in my forebears which I never felt when I was young. In psycho-analysis I was led to think no further back than to my childhood, and my relation with my father and mother. I sought the cause of my rebellion in myself, in my loves and my fears. I didn't see it as only one of a long series of rebellions stretching back into the years before I was born. An ageing clergymen had undressed himself in a field, another had left his family abruptly to seek some golden memory of a time when he was sixteen years old and alone without parents on a Caribbean island. My father and mother too must surely have rebelled, though I do not know the nature of their rebellion, unless perhaps it was in the loving folly of their marriage.

Of my grandparents, it is to my father's father that I feel the closest now. He went out to St Kitts as a boy of fourteen to join his brother in the management of his father's sugar estates, and his brother Charles died of yellow fever two years after his arrival, in 1840. William was alone on the island, in charge of the estates. It was a situation Ballantyne might have taken for one of his boys' books, though I doubt whether he would have included the legend that Charles had left thirteen children behind him when he died at the age of nineteen. William went home after a dose of yellow fever himself. We always leave too soon the Coral Islands where we have been happily wrecked, but the memories of Mount Misery with its head buried in the clouds, of the green wastes of sugar cane, the black sands of Dieppe Bay, of the little church of Christchurch outside which his brother lay under a grey slab of stone were powerful enough to draw back the middle-aged man from the family life at Bedford with eight children and enough money to live on in reasonable comfort (though the sugar estates on the distant island were producing less and less). For twenty years he had done very little, unlike his energetic brothers who had never lived a Ballantyne life—one was Governor of the Bank of England, another a Tory MP, the third a successful solicitor. William tried a little scientific farming and gave it up; he passed his examinations as a solicitor but he never practised. The only occupation he followed for any length of time was based on a place he called on his letter-heads 'Bleak House, the Plains of Desolation'.

He had become the only active (though none of his activities was very active) director of a peat company—his young partner committed suicide. He would disappear suddenly from Bedford, the large house and the large garden and the large family, leaving no money behind, and the next they would hear of him was from the overseer's hut, the only human habitation among the black bogs (which perhaps recalled the black volcanic sands of the island). He took no genuine part in the enterprise, but he would take long walks with a book in his pocket, and then return at night to the

[93]

unfinished tramway-line, the half-built hydraulic plant, the rough food, the uneducated conversation in the lamplight and the narrow camp bed. He wasn't made for the family life in Bedford, the games of clumps and snap, the exciting visit of a Mr Rust who set the girls in turmoil. There was a barrier between him and his children. He would sit alone in his study, reading and marking his books. Only his daughter Alice had something of his frustrated romantic nature which would lead her, after his death, to a career in South Africa from which she rarely returned to England with her tales of new exotic friends, Olive Schreiner and General Smuts. I can just remember her with her square kindly sensible face, turning a little masculine with age, an impression of gaberdine. At twenty-two she was writing to her brother Graham: 'When I think of the countries I want to visit, the mountains I want to climb' (her father had written a little book which was printed in St Kitts about his ascent of Mount Misery), 'the rivers, forests and valleys I want to explore, I feel half frantic at the thought that I am getting older and older and am no more likely to travel than I was ten years ago.'

Suddenly in May 1881—the worst time of year to set out to the Caribbean—my grandfather decided to pack up and leave. Graham saw him off in London and wrote to his mother: 'Did father send you a line from Southampton? I left him at 1 a.m. on Tuesday morning at the Charing Cross Hotel, endeavouring to finish a large cigar. He told me he intended to take very little rest that night, as he wished to be very sleepy on the following, the first night on board. I hope this plan succeeded but I have strong misgivings thereon. If the sea was rough in addition to the seasickness he would have all the additional discomfort of weariness. Our theatre was, after all, badly chosen. We went to *The Lady of Lyons*. A most mournful piece, not at all calculated to raise the spirits of an intending voyageur.'

He wasn't much missed, judging from Alice's letters to her brother Graham in London. Life in Bedford was as exciting as ever, with birthday treats and excursions and tea in the garden and walks by moonlight and the seductive behaviour on a tricycle at Barford of my other grandfather's curate, Mr Humble, and a further visit from the alarming Mr Rust ('He is so utterly inscrutable in his looks, words and deeds, that I know no more what his feelings are than if he were the Sphynx').

In spite of her longing for adventure, when the chance came Alice turned it firmly down. 'Thank you so very much, dear Papa, for your wish to have Florence and me with you for a time, but indeed, indeed, it cannot be. It was so very good of you to propose it that it seems ungrateful to refuse it point blank, but I really could not go unless we all went too. Like Mama, I do not like the thought of you being all alone; it seems so dreary for you. But as Mama, I suppose, has written to you all the Pros and Cons for your projects, I think I need not say any more, except to hope that we shall all meet again somewhere or other.' 'Somewhere or other', it must have seemed a chilling phrase to the middle-aged man who had failed to relive his youth under Mount Misery. Less than two months' later he was dead of fever.

His grave is the same shape and size as his brother's, but he has failed to leave any impression on the island among all the coloured Greenes. It is Charles, dead at nineteen, forty-one years earlier, who is remembered. Perhaps the legend of his thirteen children is not wholly untrue, for when I visited the island two years ago, in the features of one would-be cousin I thought I saw a close resemblance to my Uncle Graham.

2

I don't know by what process of elimination my father and brother chose Kenneth Richmond to be my analyst, but it was a choice for which I have never ceased to be grateful, for at his house in Lancaster Gate began what were perhaps the happiest six months of my life. Active happiness depends to some extent on contrast—a lovers' meeting would not be the same without the days of deprivation, and those breakfasts in bed on a tray neatly laid, brought by a maid in a white starched cap, followed by hours of private study under the trees of Kensington Gardens, seemed all the more miraculous after the stone steps, the ink-stained schoolroom, the numbering-off at the bogs, the smell of farts around the showers. And London was there just down the road. I was independent. I could take a bus or tube to any destination. Films and theatres depended only on the management of my pocket-money. There were no Sunday walks in unwanted company. I was growing rapidly into an adult without the torments of puberty.

Only once something happened to disturb the quiet and restful routine. A guest was describing an accident at dinner, and my mind went back to Harston ten years before, a story of two ladies on the Royston road in a carriage: the horse had run away, and one had fallen out and her long hat-pin had pierced her brain. I found myself on the dining-room floor. I had fainted as sometimes I had fainted at early service in the school chapel. I wasn't worried; my imagination had a way of showing me the details of an accident though they were never described, and then I would faint like a medical student at an operation. I was surprised when Richmond took me to a specialist in Harley Street, but I thought no more of it. The incident was forgotten for four years.

Often of an evening I found myself in the company of authors. Richmond himself was one, if only of a book which I found rather dull reading, on educational theory. Walter de la Mare came to the house—the poet I admired most at that time—and wrote his spidery signature in my new-bought copy of *The Veil*. Often with him was his close friend, Naomi Royde-Smith, the editor of the *Weekly Westminster*, who had published Rupert Brooke's early poems; she was too kind to me, so that a year later I began to bombard her with sentimental fantasies in poetic prose (she even published some of them). J. D. Beresford came too—a novelist crippled by infantile paralysis. *The Hampdenshire Wonder* remains one of the finest and most neglected novels of this period between the great wars, although it was an inferior novel, *Revolution*, which appealed more to me then. One evening we played a game in which each guest in turn had to imitate a vegetable, and I remember how we all simultaneously recognized de la Mare's stick of asparagus. Such evenings were far away from the hours of prep in St John's musty schoolroom. My only duties were to read history of a morning in Kensington Gardens and at eleven o'clock to go in for an hour's session with the analyst.

Kenneth Richmond had more the appearance of an eccentric musician than anyone you might suppose concerned with curing the human spirit. A tall stooping figure in his early forties, he had a distinguished musician's brow with longish hair falling behind without a parting and a face disfigured by large spots which must have been of nervous origin. There were two little girls who were brought up on the principle that children should never be thwarted, with the result that they were almost unbearably spoilt. On Sundays I was left in charge of them for an hour, while Richmond and his beautiful wife Zoe went to a church in Bayswater of some esoteric denomination, where the minister asked the congregation to decide by vote whether they would prefer that evening a sermon or a lecture on a psychological subject. Meanwhile at home I was seeing to it that for one hour a week the children learnt what it was to be thwarted.

I kept perforce a dream diary (I have begun to do so again in old age), and fragments of the dreams I can remember still, though the diary has been destroyed for nearly half a century. There was one dream of which I remember colours of great beauty; there were towers and pinnacles which might have come out of Miss Nesbit's *The Enchanted City*, and I heard a bodiless voice intoning, 'Princess and Lord of Time, there are no bounds to thee'; and I remember a nightmare in which I was pursued by sinister Chinese agents and took shelter in a hut with an armed detective, but, just as I felt the relief of security in his company, I looked at the hand holding the revolver and saw that he had the long nails of a Chinaman.

Sitting in Kensington Gardens, reading of the Carolingians in a dull blue volume of Tout, I kept one eye alert for possible adventures among the nursemaids, but the only adventure I had was not of the kind I desired. An elderly man, with an old Etonian tie and a gaze unhappy and shifty, drew a chair up to mine and started to talk of schools. Was there corporal punishment at my school, and did I suppose there were any schools left where girls were whipped? He had an estate, he told me, in Scotland, where everyone went around in kilts, so convenient in some ways, and perhaps I would like to come for a holiday there ... Suddenly he sloped away, like a wind-blown umbrella, and I never saw him again.

When eleven struck in a Bayswater church tower I would cross the road, turn a corner and go into the little house in Lancaster Gate. If I couldn't remember the last night's dream I would be asked to invent one (for some reason if I invented a dream it always began with a pig). Richmond belonged to no dogmatic school of psycho-analysis, so far as I can make out now: he was nearer to Freud than Jung, but Adler probably contributed. There had been a tragedy twenty years before when a patient had killed himself and the coroner had been brutally unsympathetic, and I have the impression that he proceeded very carefully, very tentatively. My life with him did me a world of good, but how much was due to the analysis and how much to the breakfasts in bed, the quiet of Kensington Gardens, the sudden independence of my life I would not like to say, nor whether the analysis went deep enough. In any case, as Freud wrote, 'much is won if we succeed in transforming hysterical misery into common unhappiness'.

There he would always be, sitting behind the desk with his marred musician's face, stop-watch ready, waiting for my coming. Was there a couch, the stock-subject of so many jokes? I can't remember. I would begin to read out my dream, and he would check my associations with his watch. Afterwards he would talk in general terms about the theory of analysis, about the mortmain of the past which holds us in thrall. Sometimes, as the analysis progressed, he would show little hints of excitement—as though he scented something for which he had been waiting for a long while. But so far as my own dreams and associations went, he *told* me nothing; he patiently waited for me to discover the long road back for myself. I too began to feel the excitement of the search. Perhaps, in spite of all the good it did me, the excitement was too heady for a boy and fostered the desire to turn up every stone to discover what lay beneath, to question motives, to doubt—no love would be simple afterwards or free from dusty answers.

The classic moment approached, as in all such analyses,

when the emotion of the patient is due to be transferred: a difficult period for the analyst. Perhaps Richmond was trying to provide a subject away from home, for one of the evening callers proved to be a girl who was a ballet-student and one night we went to see her dance. With the added glamour of the stage around her, I nearly fell in love. Exploring London I had found a little bookshop on the Embankment near Albert Bridge and I bought a first edition for a few shillings of Ezra Pound's early romantic poems, *Personae*—he displaced Walter de la Mare in my admiration. So, under the influence of *Personae*, I wrote three sentimental imagist lines to the girl, whose romantic name was Isola ('a future Pavlova' I wrote to my mother), but I never showed them to her, the relation never went further, and I did not see her again. The transference took a more inconvenient route, settling on my analyst's wife, and the moment I feared at last arrived when, sitting in Kensington Gardens, I found the only dream I had to communicate was an erotic one of Zoe Richmond. For the first time I dreaded the hour of eleven. I could, of course, say that I remembered nothing, and Richmond would tell me to invent, and I could trot out the habitual pig, but I was caught sufficiently by the passion for analysis to be repelled at the thought of cheating. To cheat was to behave like a detective who deliberately destroys a clue to murder. I steeled myself and left the Gardens and went in.

'And now,' Richmond said, after a little talk on general theory, 'we'll get down to last night's dream.'

I cleared my dry throat. 'I can only remember one.'

'Let's have it.'

'I was in bed,' I said.

'Where?'

'Here.'

He made a note on his pad. I took a breath and plunged.

'There was a knock on the door and Zoe came in. She was naked. She leant over me. One of her breasts nearly touched my mouth. I woke up.'

'What's your association to breasts?' Richmond asked, setting his stop-watch.

'Tube train,' I said after a long pause.

'Five seconds,' Richmond said.

Towards the end of my stay with the Richmonds my rich Greene uncle, Eppy, who perhaps did not wish to be out-done by his intellectual brother, sent his elder daughter Ave to be analysed, and she too stayed in the house. Perhaps if she had come a little sooner my transference would have been directed towards her, for she was a very pretty girl, who, a few years later, was courted by all the Greene brothers, except Hugh who was still too young. Herbert and I particularly entered into rivalry. Tennis on summer even-ings, exciting car-rides to the King's Arms in the neigh-bouring town of Tring . . . there were even moments when my German aunt became worried: another first-cousin marriage in the Greene family would have been a disaster. Now in London with all the opportunities open nothing occurred. In those days at sixteen a boy was still very young. With daring I took her to the first London production of Eugene O'Neill's *Anna Christie* (her family, I learnt afterwards, considered it an unsuitable choice). I was still so heartfree that I could wonder, with cynical amusement, how long it would be before her emotions began to be transferred towards our bizarre and spotty analyst. But I was not there to see. Before that happened (if it ever did) I was returned—repaired—to the world of school.

Chapter 5

I

It was a life transformed. I was no longer a boarder at that hated brick barracks called St John's, which had become so mysteriously changed from the home of a happy childhood, and I had no fear of the old routine of classes. Classes, when once I had outwitted and outgrown the gym, I had never hated, and I returned to them with the proud sense of having been a voyager in very distant seas. Among the natives whom I had encountered there, I had been the witness of strange rites and gained a knowledge of human nature that it would take many years for my companions to equal, or that was what I believed. Had my grandfather returned to England from the long morning rides among the sugar-canes and the black labourers of St Kitts with the same exhilarating and unbalanced sense of superiority? I had left for London a timid boy, anti-social, *farouche*: when I came back I must have seemed vain and knowing. Who among my fellows in 1921 knew anything of Freud or Jung? That summer I invited Walter de la Mare to a strawberry-tea in the garden with my parents. He had come to lecture in Berkhamsted and I posed proudly as the poet's friend, though I wished my father had been more impressed by his poetry. 'It lacks passion,' he argued with me, and to refute him I showed him a poem in *The Veil*.

> 'Poor hands, poor feeble wings,
> Folded, a-droop, O sad!
> See, 'tis my heart that sings
> To make thee glad.

> 'My mouth breathes love, thou dear.
> All that I am and know
> Is thine. My breast—draw near:
> Be grieved not so!'

He shook his head sadly, remembering Browning. 'Tenderness,' he said, 'not passion.'

I found it easy now to make friends. The domination of Carter was over for good. He belonged to another geological age, a buried stratum of school society. A school has many backwaters, but I was at last in the main stream. Instead of those petty gangsters of St John's there were Eric Guest (later a distinguished Metropolitan magistrate), Claud Cockburn, Peter Quennell. I escaped in company with Quennell the loathsome O.T.C. on condition that we both took riding lessons from the gym master, an agreeable red-faced ex-cavalryman called Sergeant Lubbock. I was always a frightened rider and later, when I had left school, I would take a horse out only in order to scare myself with jumps on the Common and escape the deep boredom which I had begun to suffer, a belated effect of the psycho-analysis, or so

I believed then, not knowing it would pursue me all my life. Quennell always rode a far more spirited horse than mine, galloped faster, jumped higher. Sometimes returning at a walk down the long road from the Common—the road of my escape—we would pass on a hot summer's day the sweating trudging ranks of the O.T.C., singing a gloomy military song, 'We're here because we're here because we're here,' like a line of Gertrude Stein, and I felt the same compassionate contempt a cavalryman must have felt in the old days for the poor bloody infantry. I no longer ride, but the smell of a horse's coat brings back at once the sense of pride and tension.

Now that I had reached the VIth form, work too was transformed. The School Certificate had been safely gained, and I was able to drop mathematics, Latin and Greek and choose the so-called modern side, with French, History and English as the main subjects. There were not many of us and we enjoyed frequent blank periods when we worked alone in the library—beneficiaries from the white cards of my father's Scheme. French, which I never learnt properly to speak, became a fascinating literary language taught by a handsome tawny-faced man called Rawes who had his roots, so it was said, in Portugal and the wine trade and wore in his button-hole the small green ribbon of a Portuguese decoration, for he had served with the unfortunate Portuguese troops who had been whipped, like porkers to an abattoir, to the mass slaughter of the Western Front. Most boys were frightened by his worldly good looks, his air of military authority, and he was unpopular, but I always enjoyed his teaching, and during his French lessons, when we would spend a whole hour juggling with words in an attempt to translate two or three lines of Molière or a sestet of Heredia, he opened my eyes to the importance of precision in my own language as well.

It was he who introduced me to Lytton Strachey's *Landmarks in French Literature*, and through Strachey I at least imagined for a while that I had become a lover of Racine. How cunningly Strachey went about his persuasion: 'The ordinary English reader today probably thinks of him—if he thinks of him at all—as a dull, frigid, conventional writer.' No boy worth his salt could fail to respond to that challenge, and on long solitary walks—which were for pleasure now and not an escape from cricket, for Kenneth Richmond had made sure that I would be excused all games—I carried *Bérénice* in my pocket in place of *The Epic of Hades*.

It was now I began to develop a love for the landscape around Berkhamsted which never left me, so that Chesterton's rather inferior political ballade '*Of the First Rain*' moves me still like poetry with its key-line: 'A storm is coming on the Chiltern Hills.' Chenies, Ivinghoe, Aldbury have always meant more to me than Dartmoor or the fells of Yorkshire, and the hidden spots of the Chilterns were all the dearer because they were on the very borders of Metroland. They had the excitement of a frontier. There was one dried stream-bed, half hidden in bushes, called the Woe Water because the stream only ran before a war. It ran before the Boer War and in July 1914. I visited it during the crisis of Munich and it was dry, but I failed to return in September

1939. The depth of this country was vertical rather than horizontal, so that a Green Man might be seen dressed in leaves only a few feet away from the school playing-fields, and once talking to a railway porter in a public house near the station I learned that he had not been as far as the High Street five hundred yards away since his wife died fifteen years before. Berkhamsted always reminds me of Rilke's poem, where beyond 'the narrow-chested' suburban houses 'a shepherd leans against the last lamp-post in the gloom'.

It was strange that, while I carried Racine with me on my walks and Ruskin's *Sesame and Lilies*, I was beginning to write the most sentimental fantasies in bad poetic prose. One abominable one, called *The Tick of the Clock*, about an old woman's solitary death, was published in the school magazine. I cut out the pages and posted them to the *Star*, an evening paper of the period, and for God knows what reason they published the story and sent me a cheque for three guineas. I took the editor's kindly letter and the complimentary copy up to the Common, and for hours I sat on the abandoned rifle-butts reading the piece aloud to myself and to the dark green ocean of gorse and bracken. Now, I told myself, I was really a professional writer, and never again did the idea hold such excitement, pride and confidence; always later, even with the publication of my first novel, the excitement was overshadowed by the knowledge of failure, by awareness of the flawed intention. But that sunny afternoon I could detect no flaw in *The Tick of the Clock*. The sense of glory touched me for the first and last time.

Then I attempted the theatre: first, modestly enough, with one-act plays, very tragic and very brutal, set in the Middle Ages, which seemed to give scope to my poor brand of poetic prose. I was much under the influence of Maurice Hewlett and *The Forest Lovers*, and many an Isoult La Desirous found her way into the plays. 'A slim girl, somewhat under the common size of the country, and overburdened with a curtain of black hair; and a sullen, brooding girl who says little, and that nakedly and askance; and in a pale face two grey eyes a-burning.' So the Abbot of Holy Thorn described her, and it was much the same character which attracted me when I read over and over again Maeterlinck's *Pelléas and Mélisande*.

Then another influence succeeded Hewlett. I went to see Lord Dunsany's *If* in which Henry Ainley played the leading part (I had myself played the Poet in Dunsany's *Lost Silk Hat* at a school fête and felt myself his colleague). Immediately afterwards I began to write a fantastic play of which I cannot even remember the title. It celebrated what I liked to believe was the sense of poetry inherent in the ceremony of afternoon tea. In 1920 tea was still one of the important meals of the day, and the most aesthetic. The silver pot, the tall tiered cake-stand, like a Chinese temple, two kinds of bread and butter, white and brown, cucumber and tomato sandwiches cut razor-thin, scones, rock-buns, and then all the cakes—plum, madeira, caraway seed—the meal had about it the lavishness of a Victorian dinner. My play, I don't know why, except that Dunsany's had taken much the same road, moved from London to Samarkand.

I sent the play to one of the many dramatic societies which existed in 1920, though I didn't fly so high as the Stage Society, and I was excited to receive a letter signed with a woman's name accepting it for production. So up I went to London one morning to meet my first management. The address was somewhere in St John's Wood, a district which in those days still retained the glamour of illicit love-nests. There was a long delay, after I sounded the bell, and when at last the door was opened, it was by an over-blown rosy woman holding a dressing-gown together, who was watched from the end of the passage by a naked man in a double bed. She looked with astonishment at my blue cap with a school crest while I explained that I had come about my play. Then she gave me a cup of rather weak Mazawattee tea (very different from the tea which I had been celebrating) and she became carefully vague, as she scrutinized me, about casting and the date of production. I don't remember that I ever heard from her again, and the society, I am sure, soon ceased to exist. Perhaps my play was the last piece of wreckage at which she clutched, and down with it sank all her dreams of some rich sucker who would put up the expenses, incidental and accidental, of his play (including the quarter's rent and the milk bill and all that went with the double bed at the end of the passage).

Still my play had been accepted. Disillusion came gently, slowly, with no letters in the day's post bearing a London postmark, and I suppose it was then I began to have the dream which continued intermittently for twenty years. In the dream, though still at school, I was an established writer who was making enough money to support himself. Why should I fear examinations when I could simply, by an act of will, abandon all study? What did a university matter to me? Why should I bother about the future and that ugly Anglo-Saxon word of double meaning a 'job'? But in waking life the classes continued without interruption, and the menace of scholarship examinations loomed ahead.

2

For English my father took charge of some of the classes, 'Dicker' Dale of others. Dicker's were the more unexpected. He would read aloud to us, a class of half a dozen only, works which were not on the syllabus, introducing us in his lazy drawl—'it's all experience'—to Beddoes and *Death's Jest-Book*. But perhaps my father's lessons drove deeper roots. He was an unconventional teacher. His three subjects were English, History and the Latin classics, and they often overlapped, so that a lesson on Robert Browning might well turn into a discussion of Trevelyan's history of Garibaldi's campaigns. The amusement and respect which he inspired in the VIth form (far, far distant now were the jeers of Carter and his immature gang who didn't know a thing about the Freudian interpretation of dreams) have been described by Claud Cockburn. 'Nobody but a fool could fail to enjoy a history lesson with Charles Greene. "Speaking", he would say, "of Rome, let me draw your attention to yesterday's events in Paris. Let me draw your attention for a moment, if I may, to the probable—nay, assured—consequences of the machinations of Mr Lloyd George and M. Clemenceau. Let us gaze for a moment into the abyss which now opens before the feet of liberal Europe. Let us not for a moment hesitate to recognize the consequences of the evil acts of these misguided men. And with this in mind, let us return to a thoughtful consideration of the situation which faced Cicero (a shady character) and his associates at the moment of the Catiline conspiracy."'

A letter written to me by Peter Quennell after I had reached Oxford describes my father's manner as he lay, almost on his back, in his deep chair at the end of the table in the library, his mortar-board at a perilous angle (he was never during school hours without gown and mortar-board and it was a shock sometimes to encounter him in his uniform on the home side of the green baize door: it was like a breach of neutrality). I had gone to Oxford a term or two in advance of Quennell carrying with me his introduction to a girl much older than either of us who lived at Boar's Hill. Greatly daring, Claud Cockburn and I invited her to lunch and I sent Quennell what must have been a rather boastful telegram (not that there was anything at all to boast about, for in a letter to my mother I wrote, 'She was very charming, but on the wrong side of twenty'). This was his reply, arranged somewhat in the *vers libre* manner of his *Masque of The Three Beasts* which was about to be published by the Golden Cockerel Press. (The poem had already appeared in *Public School Verse*, and it was said that in the school baths he had been sometimes pursued by his own particular

Carters who mockingly recited what seemed to them his
loony lines.)

My dear Graham,
  Even ironic laughter wants a fine sprinkling of discretion.
Next time you take my dear Violet out to lunch you must
arrange not to wire to me during your father's period . . .
  Your father was in the middle of what I think was an
English period. It had become rather historical. The dear
old gentleman was lying comfortably on his back—like an
inverted turtle.
      —Have you noticed how like a very dear old
        turtle he is becoming?—
      —and we had become gloomy but sonorous—
        over the future of Democracy
    And then of course entered Mrs Edmunds* (Mr Edmunds
has a new bluff sea captain macintosh which makes him look
like a statue waiting to be unveiled
      —and once wore a souwester with it)
      —in a tottering hurry
  And your father stopped in the middle of a more than
Ciceronian period
      —and heavy gloom and foreboding fell
    upon everybody—
      —and especially Peter when he heard
    it was for him—
      —and I pictured my father run over in

* My father's widowed secretary who had married, for the second
time; her new husband was a big humourless master in the Junior
School. By her first husband, with a more glamorous Irish name, she
had a beautiful daughter with long golden hair falling below her waist.
How often I walked up the long High Street almost as far as Northchurch and the Crooked Billet in the hope of catching sight of her. I
think not one of us liked the idea of poor Edmunds as her stepfather.
He seemed like an intruder on the realms of romance.

Theobald's Road
  or my Cockerel at his last gasp
And your father made ineffectual efforts to sit up and
said in a severe and entirely cold and disapproving way that
I might read it at 12
  —and—suddenly relenting—if I was good—that I
might read it now—and immediately and at once
          lest there was an answer
And I read it in icy stillness and while I was still glaring at it
  —in astonishment of mind
  —almost alarm—
your father
  asked in a yet more disapproving way if there was an
answer
  but there wasn't
And he slid back to the turtle position
  and the Ciceronian period went on—and the Demo-
cracy of Europe and its fate rolled up again like storm clouds.

Literature can have a far more lasting influence than religious teaching, and my father's enthusiasm for Robert
Browning was the bacillus of a recurring fever. The edition
I still possess of the poems was given me by him as a Confirmation present, but it was certainly not a belief in God
that Browning confirmed. I had emerged from my psycho-
analysis without any religious belief at all, certainly no belief
in the Jesus of the school chapel, and what I took from
Browning my father might well have thought unhealthily
selective. To recall today any phrase from the Sermon
on the Mount I must open the New Testament to find the
words, but some lines of Browning have stayed in my
memory for fifty years and have influenced my life more
than any of the Beatitudes:

[114]

'Better sin the whole sin, sure that God observes;
Then go live his life out! Life will try his nerves,
When the sky, which noticed all, makes no disclosure,
And the earth keeps up her terrible composure.'

'I never saw a brute I hated so;
He must be wicked to deserve such pain.'

'And the sin I impute to each frustrate ghost
Is—the unlit lamp and the ungirt loin,
Though the end in sight was a vice, I say.'

And if I were to choose an epigraph for all the novels I
have written, it would be from *Bishop Blougram's Apology*:

'Our interest's on the dangerous edge of things.
The honest thief, the tender murderer,
The superstitious atheist, demi-rep
That loves and saves her soul in new French books—
We watch while these in equilibrium keep
The giddy line midway.'

With Robert Browning I lived in a region of adulteries, of
assignations at dark street corners, of lascivious priests and
hasty dagger thrusts, and of sexual passion far more heady
than romantic love. Did my father, under that potent spell,
not even notice the meaning of the lines he read us? Even in
Swinburne I never felt so strongly the drive of desire—the
sudden exact detail which could stir a boy physically.

[115]

'What is the use of the lips' red charm,
  The heaven of hair, the pride of the brow,
  And the blood that blues the inside arm?'

'Oh, that white smallish female with the breasts . . .'

'Your soft hand is a woman of itself,
  And mine the man's bared breast she curls inside.'

'Was a lady such a lady, cheeks so round and lips so red,
  On her neck the small face buoyant, like a bell-flower
                                        on its bed,
  O'er the breast's superb abundance where a man might
                                        base his head?'

                          '. . . . there you stand,
  Warm too, and white too: would this wine
Had washed all over that body of yours,
  Ere I drank it, and you down with it, thus!'

After an afternoon of Browning it was not to Tennyson's
poems that one turned for a comparison: one walked up the
High Street in the fading light, hoping to see a tress of gold
hair dangling waist-deep.

  '——Ah, but the fresher faces! "Is it true"
  Thou'lt ask, "some eyes are beautiful and new?
  Some hair,—how can one choose but grasp such
                                        wealth . . . ?"'

In Browning there was the sense of danger, adventure, change: we could leave dull fidelity to the *Lord of Burleigh* and *Sir Galahad*.

As we grow old we are apt to forget the state of extreme sexual excitement in which we spent the years between sixteen and twenty. There was a musical comedy in the early twenties called *The Cabaret Girl*, in which Miss Dorothy Dickson starred. Today it would seem, I suppose, as comic as *The Boy Friend*, but, during my first year after leaving school, I saw it six times, and every time but one in a state of continuous physical excitement. (That one time an understudy had taken Miss Dickson's part.) There is a short story of Sean O'Casey's called 'I Wanna Woman' which is more in the mood of adolescence than romances of calf-love.

We lived in those years continuously with the sexual experience we had never known; we talked, we dreamt, we read, but it was always there, and yet, when I came to write, it was sentimental verse or sentimental prose fantasies which leaked from the pen. And in between the periods of sexual excitement came agonizing crises of boredom. Boredom seemed to swell like a balloon inside the head; it became a pressure inside the skull: sometimes I feared the balloon would burst and I would lose my reason. Then, if it were not term-time, I would beg my brother Raymond to take the train with me to London, an hour away (a workman's return ticket, if one caught an early enough train, cost only about three shillings). We would have lunch in a restaurant in Soho (a five-course half-crown lunch at Pinoli's) and walk down Charing Cross Road looking at the second-hand books. I was soothed by the movements of the crowd and the hard resistance of the pavement under my feet. A country walk in those moods was no solution. Turf yields like a body and the feel of it brought the fever back. Every haystack was the possible scene of bucolic love.

Alcohol began to appeal to me in the innocent form of bitter beer. I was offered beer first by Lubbock, my riding master, whom I visited one evening in summer. I hated the taste and drank it down with an effort to prove my manliness, and yet some days later, on a long country walk with Raymond, the memory of the taste came back to taunt my thirst. We stopped at an inn for bread and cheese, and I drank bitter for the second time and enjoyed the taste with a pleasure that has never failed me since. I had found another alleviation of the boredom-sickness and later at Oxford it served me dangerously well, when for a whole term I was drunk from breakfast till bed.

What a mess those inexperienced years can be! Lust and boredom and sentimentality, a frightened longing for the prostitute in Jermyn Street, where there were real brothels in those days, an unreal romantic love for a girl with a tress of gold and a cousin who played tennis when it was almost too dark to see the ball—in that twilight world of calf-love any number of girls can rehearse simultaneously a sentimental part which never reaches performance. My younger brother and sister had a nurse who ill-treated them and fancied me. I felt a traitor to them every evening when I came and kissed her good-night. Like a promise of something further she gave me my first razor, but the promise

[118]

was not fulfilled. One night when I came up to the nursery before bed I found my mother there, and, to show that I was not ashamed of what I did on other occasions, I went and kissed the nurse quite openly on the lips. I was neither in love nor in lust, and I was glad enough when soon after that she went away, and the children were relieved of her tyranny.

3

I went up to Oxford for the autumn term of 1922 to Balliol* with nothing resolved—a muddled adolescent who wanted to write but hadn't found his subject, who wanted to express his lust but was too scared to try, and who wanted to love but hadn't found a real object. I tried to make my aunt Maud into an intermediary between me and the girl with the gold hair, for I was afraid to write to her at home where the letter might be seen by her formidable stepfather, but my aunt after passing her one letter refused to pass another and I don't think I ever received a reply. At the same time I preserved carefully a postcard from my cousin who was somewhere in Germany, and after a little while I tried to persuade myself that I was in love with a young waitress at the George in the Cornmarket who corresponded with me

* I had failed to win a scholarship, so why to Balliol? I think my father wisely plumped for a college which at that period was anti-athletic. Also the number of students there, as in a great city, offered the shelter of anonymity.

during my first vac and sent me a snapshot. This correspondence too I preserved, making thus a harem out of
scraps of paper.

'For love of Love or from heart's loneliness . . .' No one
has better expressed than Rupert Brooke in his adolescent
verse this state of confused, half-expressed sexuality.

'Pleasure's not theirs, nor pain. They doubt, and sigh . . .'
But the genuine pain was not far off: it is possible to grow
up between one blink of the eyelids and another.

Chapter 6

I

It must have been the summer of 1923 that I reluctantly joined my family at Sheringham on the Norfolk coast. I was allowed two hundred and fifty pounds a year by my over-burdened father—a generous enough allowance in those days—and I was able, soon after I went up to Oxford, to reduce the cost to him by winning a history exhibition of fifty pounds. I had twice failed for a scholarship while at school, and I doubt whether my history had much improved in the intervening months, but we still lived in a world of influential friends. My tutor, Kenneth Bell, was an old pupil and disciple of my father's and a governor of my school. I learned from him later that the history exhibition had been awarded mainly on my English essay. 'That poem you quoted,' he said, 'I told them you had written it yourself.' He must have known that I was trying to write poetry, but the poem in fact was one by Ezra Pound which I knew by heart. 'It's the white stag, Fame, we're hunting...' Few dons in 1923 had read Pound, and, when I told Kenneth Bell of his mistake, he was not unduly disturbed. The exhibition had to go to someone: better me than another.

Perhaps if I could have saved enough money I would have gone to France that summer and not to Sheringham. Paris at the time lured me more than Athens or Rome. In Paris *Ulysses* had just been published: at the Sphynx, they said, the customers were served by naked waitresses: the Folies Bergère and the Concert Mayol were not regarded as the family entertainments they have since become. But the end of my first year saw me heavily in debt: so many barrels of beer, so many books, shelf upon shelf of them, which had nothing to do with work. At Blackwell's bookshop credit seemed to a newcomer endless (though they liked a little bit sometimes on account), but drinks were ordered through the college buttery and appeared on battels, as college bills were called (there was no credit given there), and as I spent my first two terms in lodgings in Beechcroft Road, far up in north Oxford, there had often been taxis at midnight— which left a deficit for the term ahead. So gloomily, I thought, 'It must be Sheringham this summer', for there I could live at my family's expense.

The younger children, Elisabeth and Hugh, had grown too old for a nurse, and so my kissing-instructress had not been replaced, but instead a governess had been appointed, a young woman of about twenty-nine or thirty—ten years or more older than myself. During the first days at Sheringham she made little impression—my day-dreams were still of my cousin and of the waitress at the George. My brother and sister were happy, I noticed, with her, and she joined cheerfully in our games of cricket on the sands. The first time I looked at her with any interest was at the same instant the *coup de foudre*. She was lying on the beach and her skirt had worked up high and showed a long length of naked thigh.

Suddenly at that moment I fell in love, body and mind. There was no romantic haze around this love, no make-believe: I couldn't share it like calf-love with a waitress at the George.

It is strange how vivid the memory has remained, so that I can see the stretch of beach, my mother reading, the angle from which I examined her body, and yet I cannot even remember the first time I kissed her or the hesitations and timidities which surely must have preceded the kiss. For her it was a flirtation which at first, before she scented danger, must have helped the passage of the boring hours, alone in the big nursery at Berkhamsted with two children as companions. For me it was an obsessive passion: I lived only for the moments with her. She began soon to be a little scared of what was happening; every evening of the winter vacation I would go upstairs to the nursery where she sat alone and the slow fire consumed the coals behind an iron guard. My parents must have heard my footsteps night by night as they crossed the floor, just as when I sat below I could hear her movements on the ceiling while I pretended to read. Sometimes during the day she would enlist my sister's aid to hide from me. I took dancing lessons in order to please her, and on Saturday nights we would go together to what were called 'hops' at the King's Arms. To keep up appearances I would have to dance occasionally with some boring wife of a master at the school and surrender her to other arms. Sometimes in the dark schoolroom out of term, on the excuse of teaching my brother and sister to waltz and foxtrot, we had dances of our own

[123]

when half-kisses could be exchanged without the children seeing.

But the fear set in. She told me how she was engaged to be married to a man working for Cables & Wireless in the Azores. She had not seen him for over a year, and he had become like a stranger to her. Soon he would be returning, and she would have to leave Berkhamsted to marry him. Once when she talked to me of her marriage, she wept a little. I was too inexperienced to press her for more than kisses; marriage for me seemed then to be years out of reach and there was the great difference in our ages. All I could do was urge her to break her promise and I had nothing to offer in exchange. We wrote to each other every week when I returned to Oxford, and her handwriting became so fixed in my memory that when, more than thirty years after we had ceased to write, I received a letter asking me to get her seats for my first play *The Living Room*, I recognized her hand on the envelope and my heart beat faster until I remembered that I was a man of over fifty and she, by now, well into her cruel sixties.

I can see now that my courtship from the distance of Oxford went to comic and selfish lengths. For example I organized a reading of poems by 'Oxford Poets' with what was then the British Broadcasting Company at Savoy Hill. Among others Harold Acton took part, Joseph Gordon Macleod, T. O. Beachcroft and A. L. Rowse, who was the only one to receive a 'fan' letter—it came from an old invalid lady who had found his verses, she wrote, 'consoling'. I read an extract from an attempt on the Newdigate Prize.

The subject that year was 'Lord Byron', but my sentimental blank verse lines had nothing to do with Byron—
they were directed at Berkhamsted where the governess sat
listening, as she had been warned to do. Poor young woman,
it never occurred to me what embarrassment she must have
suffered, seated before the radio set with my father and
mother. Other verses too I poured out to her like letters and
sold them to the *Weekly Westminster*, still edited by Kenneth
Richmond's friend, Miss Naomi Royde-Smith, or gave them
gratis to the *Oxford Outlook* (of which I was conveniently
the editor), or sent them to the *Oxford Chronicle*, which paid
me five shillings a poem, or the *Decachord*, which paid
nothing. There would have been no doubt at home of the
subject of my verses. Even the sound of her footsteps on the
nursery floor were recorded in plain lines, and my jealousy
of the man she was to marry. In one sonnet written in that
winter of 1924 I looked forward without relish to my
solitary future—'Eating a Lyons chop in 1930' the sonnet
pessimistically began. How could I have imagined that by
1930 I would have been already happily married for two
years? But the reality of a passion should not be questioned
because of its brevity. A storm in the shallow Mediterranean
may be over in a few hours, but while it lasts it is savage
enough to drown men, and this storm was savage. Passion
had temporarily eased the burden of boredom: hope was a
panacea, even when it was only expectation of the 'hop' at
the King's Arms on the next Saturday night, but there were
times—even a governess has holidays and days of freedom
—when I realized that my old enemy was merely biding his

moment. A manic-depressive, like my grandfather—that would be the verdict on me today, and analysis had not cured my condition.

2

I can remember very clearly the afternoon I found the revolver in the brown deal corner-cupboard in a bedroom which I shared with my elder brother. It was the early autumn of 1923. The revolver was a small ladylike object with six chambers like a tiny egg-stand, and there was a cardboard box full of bullets. I never mentioned the discovery to my brother because I had realized the moment I saw the revolver the use I intended to make of it. (I don't to this day know why he possessed it; certainly he had no licence, and he was only three years older than myself. A large family is as departmental as a Ministry.)

My brother was away—probably climbing in the Lake District—and until he returned the revolver was to all intents my own. I knew what to do with it because I had been reading a book (I think Ossendowski was the author) which described how the White Russian officers, condemned to inaction in southern Russia at the tail-end of the counterrevolutionary war, used to invent hazards with which to escape boredom. One man would slip a charge into a revolver and turn the chambers at random, and his companion would put the revolver to his head and pull the trigger. The chance, of course, was five to one in favour of life.

One forgets emotions easily. If I were dealing with an imaginary character, I might feel it necessary for verisimilitude to make him hesitate, put the revolver back into the cupboard, return to it again after an interval, reluctantly and fearfully, when the burden of boredom and despair became too great. But in fact there was no hesitation at all: I slipped the revolver into my pocket, and the next I can remember is crossing Berkhamsted Common towards the Ashridge beeches. Perhaps before I had opened the corner cupboard, boredom had reached an intolerable depth. The boredom was as deep as the love and more enduring—indeed it descends on me too often today. For years, after my analysis, I could take no aesthetic interest in any visual thing: staring at a sight that others assured me was beautiful I felt nothing. I was fixed, like a negative in a chemical bath. Rilke wrote, 'Psychoanalysis is too fundamental a help for me, it helps you once and for all, it clears you up, and to find myself finally cleared up one day might be even more helpless than this chaos.'

Now with the revolver in my pocket I thought I had stumbled on the perfect cure. I was going to escape in one way or another, and perhaps because escape was inseparably connected with the Common in my mind, it was there that I went.

Beyond the Common lay a wide grass ride known for some reason as Cold Harbour to which I would occasionally take a horse, and beyond again stretched Ashridge Park, the smooth olive skin of beech trees and last year's quagmire of leaves, dark like old pennies. Deliberately I chose my ground, I believe without real fear—perhaps because so many semi-suicidal acts which my elders would have regarded as neurotic, but which I still consider to have been under the circumstances highly reasonable, lay in the background of this more dangerous venture. They removed the sense of strangeness as I slipped a bullet into a chamber and, holding the revolver behind my back, spun the chambers round.

Had I romantic thoughts about my love? I must have had, but I think, at the most, they simply eased the medicine down. Unhappy love, I suppose, has sometimes driven boys to suicide, but this was not suicide, whatever a coroner's jury might have said: it was a gamble with five chances to one against an inquest. The discovery that it was possible to enjoy again the visible world by risking its total loss was one I was bound to make sooner or later.

I put the muzzle of the revolver into my right ear and pulled the trigger. There was a minute click, and looking down at the chamber I could see that the charge had moved into the firing position. I was out by one. I remember an extraordinary sense of jubilation, as if carnival lights had been switched on in a dark drab street. My heart knocked in its cage, and life contained an infinite number of possibilities. It was like a young man's first successful experience of sex—as if among the Ashridge beeches I had passed the test of manhood. I went home and put the revolver back in the corner-cupboard.

This experience I repeated a number of times. At fairly long intervals I found myself craving for the adrenalin drug, and I took the revolver with me when I returned to Oxford. There I would walk out from Headington towards Elsfield down what is now a wide arterial road, smooth and shiny like the walls of a public lavatory. Then it was a sodden unfrequented country lane. The revolver would be whipped behind my back, the chamber twisted, the muzzle quickly and surreptitiously inserted in my ear beneath the black winter trees, the trigger pulled.

Slowly the effect of the drug wore off—I lost the sense of jubilation, I began to receive from the experience only the crude kick of excitement. It was the difference between love and lust. And as the quality of the experience deteriorated, so my sense of responsibility grew and worried me. I wrote a bad piece of free verse (free because it was easier in that way to express my meaning clearly without literary equivocation) describing how, in order to give myself a fictitious sense of danger, I would 'press the trigger of a revolver I already know to be empty'. This verse I would leave permanently on my desk, so that if I lost the gamble, it would provide incontrovertible evidence of an accident, and my parents, I thought, would be less troubled by a fatal play-acting than by a suicide—or the rather bizarre truth. (Only after I had given up the game did I write other verses which told the true facts.)

It was back in Berkhamsted during the Christmas of 1923 that I paid a permanent farewell to the drug. As I inserted my fifth dose, which corresponded in my mind to the odds against death, it occurred to me that I wasn't even excited: I was beginning to pull the trigger as casually as I might take an aspirin tablet. I decided to give the revolver —since it was six-chambered—a sixth and last chance. I twirled the chambers round and put the muzzle to my ear for a second time, then heard the familiar empty click as the chambers shifted. I was through with the drug, and walking back over the Common, down the new road by the ruined castle, past the private entrance to the gritty old railway station reserved for the use of Lord Brownlow, my mind was already busy on other plans. One campaign was over, but the war against boredom had got to go on. I put the revolver back in the corner cupboard, and going downstairs I lied gently and convincingly to my parents that a friend had invited me to join him in Paris.

For I had to get away somehow from evenings where the ceiling of the room where I sat sounded under the well-known footsteps and all I had for physical expectations were the Saturday night 'hops' or a few minutes pressed together in the dark schoolroom. My rival was soon to return from the Azores and the governess would be married and gone before the long summer vac came round again. The whole episode of my love had lasted less than six months, but even today it seems to have endured as long as youth itself. As for the revolver I was never tempted to take it up again, but it left an influence on my night-life; in dreams even to this day I often raise a revolver to defend myself against some enemy and find it useless because, when I fire, the bullets are discharged without the force to penetrate. A kind of Russian roulette remained too a factor in my later life, so that without previous experience of Africa I went on an absurd and reckless trek through Liberia; it was the fear of boredom which took me to Tabasco during the religious persecution, to a *léproserie* in the Congo, to the Kikuyu reserve during the Mau-Mau insurrection, to the emergency in Malaya and to the French war in Vietnam. There, in those last three regions of clandestine war, the fear of ambush served me just as effectively as the revolver from the corner-cupboard in the life-long war against boredom.

Chapter 7

I

I only stayed in Paris ten days, although it was my first visit abroad. Claud Cockburn and I had become probationary members of the Communist Party at Oxford, and I held a Party card containing three or four sixpenny stamps which represented my monthly contributions. It was a very small branch, though it served both city and university; I doubt if there were more than half a dozen members, and Cockburn and I, with no scrap of Marxist belief between us, joined only with the far-fetched idea of gaining control and perhaps winning a free trip to Moscow and Leningrad, cities which six years after the Revolution still had a romantic appeal. Our mercenary motive was seen through almost at once by a very serious Australian Rhodes scholar who was much older than ourselves and we soon ceased to attend meetings.*
But I still kept my card as a souvenir, and with it in my hand I visited the Communist headquarters in Paris, where they were equally puzzled by my youth and my bad French.

* Life's ironies: neither Cockburn nor I were then at all inclined to Communism, but some years later he became a Party member and afterwards left the Party, while I found myself thirty years on, after my experience of the French Vietnamese war and American policy there, in greater sympathy with Communism than ever before, though less and less now with the Russian version of it.

However I was invited to a meeting that night somewhere around Menilmontant. The working-class quarter was full of policemen in blue steel helmets and Gardes Mobiles who carried rifles, but the meeting nonetheless bored me to exhaustion. Endless messages from branches abroad were read out amid cheers, and soon I slipped away and took the Métro home to my hotel in the Rue Tronchet and the huge blue copy of *Ulysses*, the size of a telephone directory, which I had bought on my first day in Paris at Sylvia Beach's bookshop. Years later, writing *It's a Battlefield*, I used this meeting and the sense of futility it conveyed to describe rather unfairly a branch meeting of the Communist Party in London.

This was the only experience which differentiated my visit from that of any other young man in the 1920s. I went to the Casino de Paris to see Mistinguette, to the Concert Mayol to excite myself with naked breasts and thighs, and then back to the small room smelling of urine in the second-class hotel in the Rue Tronchet, passing the Madeleine on my way. The Madeleine in those days was suitably surrounded by aunt-like figures of a certain age who called to me as I went by. But I was too timid to make my first experiment in copulation with any of them, or else they were not young or pretty enough when I compared them with the girls of the Concert Mayol. It was certainly no sense of morality which restrained me. Morality comes with the sad wisdom of age, when the sense of curiosity has withered.

I had one respectable chance of adventure, and there is a touch of vanity in the letter I wrote to my mother about it: someone at least had considered me old enough to marry. 'At the moment I am in a state of utter panic. I have just had two solid hours of French conversation (good for me, I suppose) with a French matron in this hotel. She has a daughter, whom I have not met. I did not meet the mother till this morning. She has been matchmaking in a most brazen and terrifying manner. She has described her daughter most intimately with regard to character and looks. She has even insisted on my meeting her this afternoon, and corresponding with her from England when I return. She has had the barefaced impertinence, though I assure you I gave her no encouragement, to enquire into my prospects. As though I had asked her blasted daughter in marriage! At any rate she confessed that her daughter was *plus tranquille et plus timide* than herself. And at the end, as she left the room, leaving me limp and helpless, a poor fly hopelessly entangled in the web, powerless even to struggle, she let out her only words of English, "Pardon me, but you see—I am a mozzer." It's lucky I'll be leaving on Wednesday. She can't possibly make me propose in three days. And yet—the Lord knows what she can't do.'

2

As a distraction from lost love and baffled desire Paris was not a success, and now that Russian roulette had failed me, I tried drink instead when I returned to Oxford. For nearly one term I went to bed drunk every night and began drinking again immediately I woke. I had given up going to lectures after my first term, judging them less useful than reading; and now, though I was within a few terms of my final exams, I only had to be sober once a week when I read an essay to my tutor.

At the end of term there was a ceremony called 'The Handshake', when each in turn had to sit at a table opposite the Master and the Dean, while his tutor commented on the work he had done during the term. I was helped as far as the door by two of my friends, Robert Scott and George Whitmore, who held me on a steady course through the quad. Then I slumped into a chair beside Kenneth Bell and faced the Master and the Dean. I don't think it occurred to either of these two that an undergraduate would appear before them drunk at that early hour and on such a serious occasion and they probably put down any strangeness in my manner to nerves. My tutor recognized my state, but he was sympathetic. Kenneth Bell and the Dean (who was known as 'Sligger') were the two opposite poles of the college, and they had little liking for each other. Sligger gathered around him young men who attracted him by their looks and who played, if only superficially, the comedy of homosexual inclinations: Bell's pupils were aggressively heterosexual and were inclined, like himself, to drink large quantities of beer. So he stage-managed skilfully what might have been a disastrous Handshake, and I was released safely into the care of my friends who had a taxi waiting and they lodged me as though I were something breakable in the train for Bletchley. The long wait there for the connection to

Berkhamsted was enough to sober me. I have never again in my life drunk quite so heavily over so long a period, but I have cause to be grateful to that spell of alcoholism: it left me with a strong head and a tough liver. 'Mithridates he died old.'*

3

Now I look back, there seems something a little bizarre about my Oxford days. They certainly do not recall those of Newman or the early pages of *Brideshead Revisited*; perhaps they were closer to Maclean's and Kim Philby's at Cambridge ...

A small affair of what might have become espionage began innocently enough in early 1924. I had read a book of short stories by Geoffrey Moss called *Defeat* about the occupied zones of Germany. Moss described the attempt of the French authorities in their zone to establish a separatist Palatine Republic between the Moselle and the Rhine.

* I think it must have been during this period of perpetual drunkenness that I unconsciously made an enemy who cropped up nearly twenty years later in strange circumstances. In 1942 I went up to Kailahun in Sierra Leone near the Liberian and French Guinea border to try to contact some American missionaries in Liberia who possessed a radio transmitter that might prove useful in our watch on the Vichy border. Installed in Kailahun was a district commissioner who didn't disguise his profound dislike of me. So violent did his antagonism prove that I had to have a censorship clamped on his mail, and his letters home proved to be breaking all the rules of security. I still remain in complete ignorance of what happened between us at Balliol.

German criminals had been brought in from Marseilles and other ports—pimps, brothel-keepers, thieves from French prisons—to support the collaborators. Even one of the ministers had served a prison sentence. French troops held the crowds back while unarmed German police were beaten unconscious. Only the opposition of the British and American governments put an end to what was known as the Revolver Republic, but it was believed in Germany that at any moment the 'spontaneous' outbreak would be renewed.

I was easily aroused to indignation by cruelties not my own, and the idea of experiencing a little danger made me write to the German Embassy in Carlton Gardens and offer my services as a propagandist. The *Oxford Outlook* was at my disposal, for I was the editor, and to the *Oxford Chronicle*, a city paper, I was a regular contributor, if only of the five-shilling love poems.

I had not expected the promptitude of the German response. Coming back one early evening to my rooms in Balliol I found my armchair occupied, my only bottle of brandy almost finished, and a fat blond stranger who rose and introduced himself, 'Count von Bernstorff.' He was the first secretary of the German Embassy, a man who loved luxury and boys and who frequented a shady club called the Abyssinia in Archer Street, Soho. No one could have foretold that hidden in those folds of flesh was a hero who was to run a Jewish escape-route from Germany to Switzerland during the last war and be executed in Dachau.

My days after that seemed to be filled by Germans—there

[137]

was a very pretty Countess von Bernstorff, the diplomat's cousin, who left a scented glove behind in my room to be added to my adolescent harem of inanimate objects, a young man with a long complicated title, who claimed a nobler and longer descent than the Hohenzollerns, and a mysterious wizened narrow figure with a scarred face, Captain P., whose full name I have now forgotten. Captain P. would turn up at irregular intervals, like someone who looks in at a kitchen door to see if the kettle is boiling. Now that I have worked in the Secret Service myself, I feel I should have smelt him out immediately as an intelligence officer. The day arrived when I called at Carlton Gardens and Count Bernstorff handed me a packet and told me to burn the envelope—which, of course, I kept for some years as a souvenir. Inside were twenty-five pound notes—more than sufficient in those days for a fortnight's holiday down the Rhine and the Moselle.

My father took the affair very seriously. He told me how Lord Haldane's career had been wrecked by his too great friendship for the Germans, and he offered to pay for my holiday himself. I knew that he could ill afford his generosity and I refused the offer. After all, I argued, I was not going to follow the same career as Lord Haldane and was unlikely to attain his eminence.

I asked Claud Cockburn to come with me; we were to be joined in Germany by my cousin Tooter, for neither Claud nor I could speak German. We went inexpensively by the Hook, and as we were laughing with pleasure in the railway compartment to Harwich at the thought of our free holiday

[138]

and the confiding nature of German diplomats, there slid in beside us thin narrow Captain P. with his duel-scarred face. Our laughter broke abruptly off and we tried to appear the serious observers we were meant to be. I was very sea-sick on the crossing in spite of Mothersil and saw no more of Captain P.—perhaps he was sea-sick too.

Our holiday was uneventful, in spite of the stack of introductions which waited for us in the Cologne hotel. There we met a man called Waldenheim who was the political organizer in the German Volkspartei, and an industrial magnate, Doctor Hennings, who owned a great dye factory outside Cologne and gave us a gargantuan feast in Leverkusen, while he talked glibly of Germany's starvation.

After Cologne we went to Essen and lodged in simple luxury at Krupp's private hotel. In the Ruhr, newly occupied by French troops, 'there was a delightful sensation of being hated by everybody,' I wrote my mother. 'No tourist could be expected in the Ruhr, and I suppose all foreigners are taken for French officials. In the evening we went to a cabaret where we were even more unwelcome, and a rather fat naked woman did a symbolic dance of Germany in chains, ending up of course by breaking her fetters.' I can remember still the menace of Essen where most of the factory workers were on strike: the badly lit streets, the brooding groups. We flirted with fear and began to plan a thriller together rather in Buchan's manner.

At Bonn, then a small provincial university town, we stayed for half a crown a day in a little *gasthaus* built in 1649. On the riverside at night, encouraged by the atrocity stories we had heard in Cologne, we followed innocent Senegalese soldiers in the hope of seeing a rape, which never occurred. At Trier on the Moselle, which had been the centre of the Separatist movement, Spahis in turbans and long cloaks lounged under the Roman gateway, but there were no incidents to excite us. A local editor told us that every letter which left Trier was censored by the French authorities, so I wrote a letter to myself, addressed to 'The Editor of the *Oxford Outlook*', recounting imaginary atrocities by the French and mentioning the day and hour of the train we were to take out of the zone. But there were no soldiers to arrest us on the platform and the letter arrived safely in England unopened—a useful lesson in checking one's information.

Only in Heidelberg, outside the occupied zone, did our introductions provide us with an interesting encounter. There in the bureau of what was called respectably the Society for the Relief of Exiles from the Palatinate we met a kindly middle-aged man in plus-fours called Doctor Eberlein, who frankly explained to us the real purpose of his society. He was a kidnapper. He recruited young men to drive fast cars across the frontier into the French zone where they seized mayors and officials who were collaborating with the French authorities and bundled them back into Germany to be 'tried' for high treason.

In those days, when Hitler was still unknown to us, Doctor Eberlein's adventurous story appealed to me and gave me an idea for the future. When I returned home I wrote to Count Bernstorff suggesting that there might be difficulties in transmitting funds to the secret nationalist organizations in the occupied zone. An Oxford under-graduate would hardly be suspected as a courier . . . After some delay Bernstorff replied. He wrote that at present they had no difficulty in transmitting funds, but he had been asked by his 'friends' in Berlin whether I would be prepared to return to the French zone, get in touch with the Separa-tist leaders and try to obtain some information about their plans for the future. I finished reading the letter with excite-ment and a measure of pride, for I was being promoted from propaganda to espionage. It was a heady thought for a boy of nineteen, and I am amazed now, in these more security-conscious days, at what both of us had so rashly put upon paper.

Today, I would have scruples about the purpose I served, but at that age I was ready to be a mercenary in any cause so long as I was repaid with excitement and a little risk. I sup-pose too that every novelist has something in common with a spy: he watches, he overhears, he seeks motives and analyses character, and in his attempt to serve literature he is unscrupulous.

It was an odd schizophrenic life I lived during the autumn term of 1924. I attended tutorials, drank coffee at the Cadena, wrote an essay on Thomas More, studied the revolution of 1688 'from original sources', read papers on poets to the Ordinary and the Mermaid, attended debates at the Union, got drunk with friends; then 'Cross a step or two of dubious twilight, come out on the other side, the novel'. There another life began, where I exchanged last letters with the woman I loved, who was engaged to another man, wrote a first novel never to be published, the unhappy history of a black child born to white parents, and prepared plans with Bernstorff for espionage. All the time Germans were dropping into my life unannounced, arriving from Paddington for the day to see the colleges and drink in my room. Of course my parents had no suspicion of what I was about, but surely my social life during that last year at Oxford must have surprised them a little. 'My gentleman from the Foreign Office, Berlin,' I wrote to my mother, 'was great fun. A real pre-war Prussian, but with a charming wife. In town he had been to *Primrose*, *Saint Joan* and *White Cargo* and explained the contrast in the real blood-and-iron fashion: "You must see all kinds of plays, in order to sympathize with all types of people, for only by sympathizing with them can you dominate them. It also helps in the study of their weak points." I felt all through lunch, which he gave me at the Mitre, that he was trying to discover mine. However *his* weak point was adiposity, and I quite broke his spirit and dominated him thoroughly by dragging him round Oxford at the speed of an express.' Didn't it occur to my parents that their son was keeping somewhat curious company?

Meanwhile I wrote to a right-wing journal owned by the Duke of Northumberland called *The Patriot*, which had supported the Separatist Republic, and offered to be their correspondent in Trier. As I demanded no expenses and wrote from the respectable address of Balliol they were ready to welcome articles so long as I understood, they frankly explained, that I could represent only one point of view, their own. Then I wrote to the French Embassy in London, telling them how I was visiting Trier for *The Patriot* and would be glad of any introductions they could give me. All was set, and with sufficient cunning, when the blow fell. The Dawes Plan was formulated, the Great Powers met together at some Swiss resort, agreements were reached, guarantees were given, and one insignificant recruit to the ranks of espionage was told to fall out—his services no longer required. All the lessons in German I had been taking from a maiden lady in North Oxford had been wasted time.

I often wonder what would have happened if my plans had not been aborted. Espionage is an odd profession: for some it is a vocation, with an unscrupulous purity, untouched by mercenary or even patriotic considerations—spying for spying's sake. Already I had begun to be dissatisfied with the plain gathering of fact and rumour and with its transmission to a single source; the idea of being a double agent had occurred to me. I would be certain, I thought, to learn something of my employers' interests: even the questions I had to answer would have value for the French authorities, and the honest pity which I had formerly felt for defeated Germany had died a quick death after the gormandizing in Leverkusen and the lies of the editor in Trier. Perhaps it was lucky for me that Germany was able to dispense with my services, for the life of the double agent is a precarious one.

Chapter 8

I

Perhaps, until one starts, at the age of seventy, to live on borrowed time, no year will seem again quite so ominous as the one when formal education ends and the moment arrives to find employment and bear personal responsibility for the whole future. My parents had given me everything they could possibly owe a child and more.* Now it was my turn to decide and no one—not even the Oxford Appointments Board—could help me very far. I was hemmed in by a choice of jails in which to serve my life imprisonment, for how else at twenty can one regard a career which may last as long as life itself, or at the best until that sad moment is reached when the prisoner is released, in consideration of good behaviour, with a pension?

'I've just applied for a sub-editorship on a trans-Atlantic liner,' I wrote to my mother in January 1926, but that was only the last wild throw after many failures and more than six months of virtual unemployment since I left Oxford. I

* I came down from Oxford with heavy enough debts for those days. I admitted a hundred pounds of them to my father who paid them with hardly a complaint—the rest I worked off slowly during the next year and a half.

don't even remember whether I had an answer to that particular application.

The last term before I took Finals had been filled with frustrated efforts to decide the future. I don't think my old dream of the Nigerian Navy ever led me very far, but I passed my viva for the Consular Service, having an idea of following in the footsteps of Flecker in the Levant, although in the end I never sat for the examination, for it would have entailed many months of being coached in French. I had at the time a great admiration for some of Flecker's poems and I pictured myself in a caravanserai on the Golden Road to Samarkand or sitting beside a clicking jalousie, full of self-pity and nostalgia, in a Middle Eastern seaport:

> 'Half to forget the wandering and pain,
>   Half to remember days that have gone by,
>   And dream and dream that I am home again!'

More and more the wind-vane of my inclination swung in the direction of the East. I applied here, I applied there . . .

For example there was an interview with the Asiatic Petroleum Company. Here I had been helped by my uncle, who was head of the Brazilian Warrant Agency; he had spoken on my behalf to a director. Unfortunately I found my interviewer knew all about a book of verse I had published at Oxford and he regarded this tendency of mine with deep suspicion. No one, he said, who worked with the Asiatic Petroleum Company could have outside interests. I tried hard to persuade him that my small book had been an

[145]

aberration of adolescence: now that I was mature I had outgrown literature and my only ambition was to make a success in business. When I saw that nothing was of any avail I
suggested to my mother that there might be an opening in
the company for my eldest brother Herbert to whom unemployment was like a recurring flu—at least he hadn't put
himself out of court by publishing a book.*

I had been play-acting to the director, but there was some
truth in my desire to cut away from the past. I knew I could
never be a good poet, I associated even the act of composition with unhappy love, and my first novel which I had
written while at Oxford had never found a publisher. I was
ready to wear any mask to escape from myself, and so now I
flirted with a less important business opening than Asiatic
Petroleum, and one far removed from Samarkand. The
Lancashire General Insurance Agency had opened a branch
at Oxford under a genial manager with a silky moustache
called Captain Harris who was always good for a free drink
and a doubtful joke; he was the more popular because he
had a plump blonde secretary who hinted, when she was left
for a moment without him, at all kinds of possibilities, even
a week-end in Paris. Captain Harris offered me, as soon as I
should go down, a job at three hundred and fifty pounds a
year plus commissions, which might easily, so said the
optimistic captain, amount to another eight hundred, but I
had my doubts . . . I think I must have made contact with
the captain and his girl when I offered to readers of the

* Years later he did publish one of dubious authenticity called
Secret Agent in Spain—almost a family title.

[146]

Oxford Outlook a free insurance against failure in examinations. They had only to fill in the coupon on page 37 and in case of failure they would receive a free champagne dinner for two at one of the Oxford restaurants. I suppose Captain Harris insured me against my risks. 'Of course the chief attraction of the dinner,' I wrote home, 'will be its mixed character, and as stupid females have the reputation of being the prettiest, this ought not to be negligible.'

Finals came and went with the future undecided. I managed to get a moderate second in Modern History, my only alpha being in Political Science of which I knew least, but I remembered how I had won my Balliol exhibition with the aid of a poem by Ezra Pound, and I carefully learnt by heart certain passages from authors who had not been required reading—Santayana was one of them—passages sufficiently general in idea for them to fit with a little ingenuity into almost any essay I might be required to write. I was much helped by a game we often played at Christmas called 'Noun and Question'. In this game papers were handed round on which one person would write a noun, concealing it with a fold, another a question. The papers were all reshuffled and drawn from a hat, and a player would have to reply in verse to the question he picked, introducing the noun. One might be faced by such a word as 'skyscraper' and the question 'Who is your favourite character in Shakespeare?' Compared with this game, it was child's play to insert a purple passage of Santayana on *Hamlet* into an essay on Machiavelli's *Prince*.

I never joined the Lancashire General Insurance Agency

(although, of course, I suggested it might be a suitable opening for Herbert). Instead I found myself for two weeks an employee of the British-American Tobacco Company, destined for China in two months' time.

From the first I was daunted by the great concrete slab beside the Thames, with the uniformed porter like an officer of some foreign country demanding credentials: in the lift several middle-aged men were carrying files carefully like babies. The director who interviewed me (his name, I think, was Archibald Rose) had the appearance of a senior army officer, perhaps a brigadier, in plain clothes. He was correctly dressed in dark capitalist uniform, with a well-tied bow tie, a well-groomed moustache; he had the politeness of a man speaking to his equal in age and position. He would have made a good Intelligence officer, and I have little doubt now that he belonged, however distantly, to the Secret Service. A man in his position, recruiting and controlling men for the Chinese hinterland, could hardly have escaped contact with the 'old firm', and perhaps for that reason he was not scrupulously accurate about the details of the employment. The end justified the means.

'I want university men,' he said in remarkable contrast to the director of Asiatic Petroleum, 'because they have other interests. They can stand loneliness.' It was the best chosen fly he could have attached to his hook. After one year, he said, spent in the treaty port of Shanghai, I would be appointed to some station in the interior with one other companion. The starting salary would be four hundred and fifty pounds a year. I discovered soon after joining the firm that

[148]

both these facts were inaccurate. I would have to spend at least three years in the Shanghai office and maybe longer, and the salary was three hundred and sixty pounds. What was more important to me, because of my interest in a girl at Oxford, I should not be allowed to marry for the first four years after my appointment and only then with the permission of the directors. If I threw up the job before the end of my first year, I would not only have to pay my return fare, I would have to reimburse the company for my passage out.

I went to work—if you can call it that—almost at once. I was shown into a large office like a classroom where there were rows of desks. I felt as though I were back in the Junior School—how civilized the big library table of the Sixth seemed in comparison. To make the resemblance to school even closer the new boys, some half a dozen of them, were all placed at the front of the class. Now I can remember only two of them. Mr Rose's hook had caught one other university man: he was from Cambridge, where he had played cricket for his college but had not succeeded in taking a degree. The other sat at the desk next to mine. He had been a bank clerk in Cardiff, and he insisted on playing game after game of double noughts-and-crosses, which he invariably won. He was equally knowledgeable on the subject of motor-cycles. My tutor Kenneth Bell had written of me in his recommendation, 'He is a good mixer,' and I tried to live up to this unsound judgment, but noughts-and-crosses palled rapidly. I bought two paper-bound copies of *Chinese Self-Taught* and tried to keep my companion occupied, but we made small progress.

There was absolutely no work for any of us to do. Far from being new boys who had to be bullied into learning, it seemed that we were favoured pupils who must be kept happy. We belonged to a privileged class because we were destined for China, though sometimes I felt we more closely resembled pampered prisoners who must not know the fate to which we were being led. Our passages had already been booked, and my heart sank when my companion, busily drawing his squares for yet another game, said, 'We'll be able to do this on the boat going out, won't we?' The excitements of the Forbidden City, the Boxer Rebellion, Captain Gilson's *Lost Column* faded from my imagination, and only an awful inevitability of double noughts-and-crosses took their place. Perhaps we were to be chained together, not only on the boat and on the Shanghai Bund, but in that small up-country station, which had at first seemed so romantic a prospect.

As there was no work to distract us from the enigmatic future, they gave us to read, to help pass the slow office hours, big folio ledgers, and in the pages of insignificant accounts an entry would sometimes stand sharply out: 'For burial of coolie found dead on office steps . . . Radio for son of General Chiang Kai-shek on his twenty-first birthday . . .'

The next week we were to go to the Liverpool factory for a month and watch from eight in the morning till seven at night the way cigarettes were made. Some of the older men were knowledgeable about the foreign substances which were added to the tobacco. There was no practical point so far as I could see in our stint at the factory, for we were to be concerned in all our working future in marketing cigarettes not making them.

I went to see Archibald Rose and told him of my uncertainties. He was a little impatient. After all I was being paid five pounds a week for doing nothing at all. It was time I made up my mind, one way or another. (I nearly offered my brother Herbert in my place.) Then I went back to my lodging in Chelsea and tried to go on with my second novel —I had abandoned all hope for the first.

Conrad was the influence now, and in particular the most dangerous of all his books, *The Arrow of Gold*, written when he had himself fallen under the tutelage of Henry James. I have long forgotten the details of my plot. The setting was nineteenth-century London when Carlist refugees lived around Leicester Square. A young Englishman became involved in their conspiracy. There was a girl, of course, as romantic and ill-defined as Donna Rita. The book was a greater struggle to write than the first had been, for I had now much less hope. How could I abandon the chance of being a businessman, when it seemed my only escape from the hated obsession of trying to make imaginary characters live? I went to Oxford for a week-end to confide my fears, became engaged to be married and sent a telegram to Archibald Rose telling him that I was not returning to the office. I was ashamed of my cowardice, but I couldn't bring myself to face him: I had taken ten pounds of B.A.T. money and ten pounds seemed a lot in those days.

Again I was without a future, for I had no confidence in

those five hundred words a day on single-lined foolscap. What did I know of Carlist Spain or Spain at all except from the pages of Conrad? And yet I returned to the place and period three years later with less happy results, because the book was published and can still be found in second-hand catalogues under the title *Rumour at Nightfall*. As for the London refugees my only material lay in Carlyle's *Life of John Stirling*—the one book by Carlyle which I have been able to read with pleasure.

There was the problem of money. I had dropped my allowance when I took my job and I couldn't live at home, for the house was closed and my family at the seaside. It was Sackville Street or nothing. To the young men of my generation, down from the university without work, recourse to Sackville Street was like recourse to the pawnshop in earlier days. Among the 'gentlemen's tailors' stood an office with the Dickensian name of Truman & Knightley. I have always, most unfairly, thought of the interview between David Copperfield and Mr Squeers as taking place there.

There was a Dickensian mustiness about Sackville Street in those days, in the old-established tailors' shops on either side, where prostitutes kept flats on the second floor. The office of Truman & Knightley (chief rival of the equally Dickensian Gabbitas & Thring) might have been that of an old family solicitor, with strange secrets concealed in the metal file-boxes. It was not the cream of educational aspirants which trickled through Sackville Street. I doubt if many young men ever reached Eton or Harrow with the aid of the 'partners', for a man with a first-class degree did not require their help. They were the last hope of those needing a little temporary aid. You pawned yourself instead of your watch.

I had a horror of becoming involved in teaching. It was a profession into which you could so easily slip, as my father had done, by accident. He had intended to be a barrister, had 'eaten his dinners' and taken on the job of temporary master only to tide him over a lean period. Had he been afraid of feeling the trap close, as I was now? I wanted nothing permanent, I explained in near panic, to the partner. Was there not, perhaps, some private tutoring job which was available just for the summer? He opened his file with an air of disappointment: there were certainly good opportunities, he suggested, in the coming school term, for an exhibitioner of Balliol with an honours degree. As for private tutoring I was too late in applying, such men were needed immediately the schools broke up (he whisked over page after page), there was really nothing he could offer for someone of my qualifications . . . I would hardly be interested in this (he had detached a page with the tips of his fingers), a widowed lady living at Ashover, a village in Derbyshire, who required someone to look after her son of eight during the holidays. I would not be asked to live in the house: I would have a room in a private hotel with all my meals, but there was no salary attached. When I accepted, he looked at me with disappointment and suspicion—there must be something disgracefully wrong in my background.

The position suited me, for I had the evenings free when I could work at my novel. The country was beautiful with the grey Pennines standing all around, a few wandering sheep on desolate deserted hills, loose stone walls and occasional cottages with an Irish air of dilapidation. The widow was undemanding. She didn't want her son to be overworked. A little mathematics perhaps in the morning (I had forgotten all I ever knew), a quarter of an hour of Latin (equally forgotten), some games after lunch ... I had what I thought the bright idea of teaching him a little carpentry, though I had never practised it myself. There was a large shady garden which reminded me of my uncle's at Harston with lots of out-houses in which I discovered wooden crates, nails, hammers. I suggested we should build a toy theatre. My pupil agreed readily enough: he was a boy without initiative: he was quite ready to stand around holding the nails. Unfortunately the toy theatre failed to take even a rudimentary shape, so that after two days' work I decided that what we had been making without knowing it was a rabbit hutch. He was quite satisfied, even though there was no rabbit; he was as undemanding as his mother.

Back in the private hotel, which was called Ambervale, I plodded on till dinner time, among the Carlist refugees in Leicester Square, but the oppression of boredom soon began to descend. Once on my free day I walked over the hills to Chesterfield and found a dentist. I described to him the symptoms, which I knew well, of an abscess. He tapped a perfectly good tooth with his little mirror and I reacted in the correct way. 'Better have it out,' he advised.

'Yes,' I said, 'but with ether.'

A few minutes' unconsciousness was like a holiday from

[154]

the world. I had lost a good tooth, but the boredom was for the time being dispersed*.

The only other distraction lay in the old ladies—a gay crowd who insisted on playing paper games they didn't properly understand after dinner under the direction of an elderly gentleman: 'Famous general beginning with the letter B', the sort of thing to which family life had accustomed me. They were regarded with cynical impatience by the only other young people, a pale slang-ridden schoolboy and a girl with bobbed hair who wanted a hotel flirtation. She went with me to the pub where the landlord showed us into a private room, where we sat gingerly on the edge of a table and kissed dryly, then took refuge in a half of bitter and a gin and lime. She offered me a mongrel wire-haired terrier as a souvenir, which was to be sent by rail from Leicester to Berkhamsted and was to prove the bane of my life. Later the dog played an off-stage part in a play of mine, *The Potting Shed*, and Mr Kenneth Tynan, for reasons which remain mysterious to me, believed that he represented God. At lunch I would share a table with the flapper and her fat mother because the manageress thought it would be nice for the young people to get together. The mother was too shy to talk and whinnied like a frightened horse whenever I spoke to her.

---

* André Breton once wrote to Cocteau: 'All my efforts are for the moment directed along one line: conquer boredom. I think of nothing else day or night. Is it an impossible task for someone who gives himself to it wholeheartedly? Do understand that I insist on seeing what lies on the other side of boredom.'

The afternoons were the worst, for then there was not even the pretence of lessons. When I was tired of hide-and-seek for two I invented a game of pirates which involved a lot of physical activity on the walls of the vegetable garden. Luckily my pupil fell off the wall and cut his leg. This, in the eyes of his mother, made mathematics impossible, so now I could read to him all day while he lay stretched in a deck-chair. And so my second job came slowly and un-demandingly to an end. My family returned from the sea-side, the mongrel dog, called Paddy, arrived by train in a highly nervous condition from Leicester, and I was back at square one in Berkhamsted.

2

Three months of blank days went by, and then I arrived one wet night at Nottingham and woke next morning in the un-known city to an equally dark day. This was not like a London smog; the streets were free of vapour, the electric lights shone clearly: the fog lay somewhere out of sight far above the lamps. When I read Dickens on Victorian London I think of Nottingham in the twenties. There was an elderly 'boots' still employed at the Black Dog Inn, there were girls suffering from unemployment in the lace trade, who would, so it was said, sleep with you in return for a high tea with muffins, and a haggard blue-haired prostitute, ruined by amateur competition, haunted the corner by W. H. Smith's bookshop. Trams rattled downhill through the goose-market and on to the blackened castle. Against the rockface leant the oldest pub in England with all the grades of a social guide: the private bar, the saloon, the ladies', the snug, the public. Little dark cinemas offered matinée seats for fourpence in the stalls. I had found a town as haunting as Berkhamsted, where years later I would lay the scene of a novel and of a play. Like the bar of the City Hotel in Freetown which I was to know years later it was the focal point of failure, a place undisturbed by ambition, a place to be resigned to, a home from home.

Chapter 9

I

I had come to work on the *Nottingham Journal* unpaid because no London paper would then accept an apprentice. One entered the office through a narrow stone Gothic door, stained with soot, which resembled the portal of a Pugin chapel, and the heads of Liberal statesmen stuck out above like gargoyles: on rainy days the nose of Gladstone dripped on my head as I came in. Inside was a very ancient lift with barely room for two which creaked up a rope to the editorial offices.

The subeditors were kind to me, though I cannot remember that they ever gave me any instruction. Half-way through the evening we had a sweepstake on the football results, to which each contributed threepence, and the winner would stand chips for all and pocket the change. I was unreasonably lucky, so that around eight, more often than not, I would get a breath of fresh air while I fetched the chips from a fish-stall. They were wrapped up in an old copy of the *Journal*, but never in the *Nottingham Guardian*: the *Guardian* was the respectable paper.

In the offices of the *Journal*, unlike the Asiatic Petroleum Company, I found it a positive advantage to have published a volume of verse. The editor of the weekly book-page, a

Methodist minister, was kind to me and sometimes gave me a novel to review. The *Journal* prided itself on its literary tradition: the paper might be considered vulgar but at least it was bohemian. Sir James Barrie had once been a member of the staff, and there was even a living novelist who had graduated on the *Journal* and had a house in the town. His name was Cecil Roberts, he had written a best-seller called *Scissors*, and though I had not read any of his books, I was prepared to respect anyone who had achieved publication, and publication by Heinemann at that. When I received a royal command to tea, transmitted through the chief sub-editor, I gladly went, carrying my book of verse with me.

Roberts must still have been a young man in his thirties, but to me at twenty-one he appeared already middle-aged with a high bald forehead gleaming in the tea-light. He was elegantly dressed, and to my eyes he closely resembled Mr Micawber—he carried an eye-glass on a ribbon like Cruickshank's Micawber. He contributed in his own personality to the Dickensian atmosphere of Nottingham. He was said to be the son of a local tradesman, but other rumours, which he did not seem to resent, had it that he was the illegitimate child of one of the Dukes in the Dukeries. He was certainly not in the reduced circumstances of Mr Micawber, for he told me that in the seven years since he had become independent of journalism he had saved enough to give him a settled income of four hundred pounds a year (the equivalent I suppose of some two thousand pounds today). Perhaps I looked at him with too great an envy—I could have married on four hundred a year—for he hastened to tell me how perilous the future was. (He was really Mr Micawber in reverse.) 'He's on his last legs, I think,' I wrote home. 'He was poisoned last year in Sicily, and the doctors were entirely puzzled. Creeping paralysis is starting now. I really begin to like him—the more ill he gets the less egoistic he becomes.' I am glad to record more than forty years later that Mr Roberts is still alive and writing the third volume of his autobiography.

After the first week in Nottingham I found cheap lodgings for myself and my dog Paddy in a grim grey row with a grim grey name, Ivy House, All Saints Terrace. My landlady was a thin complaining widow with a teenaged daughter, and, when my future wife, Vivien, visited me for a holiday week-end, the girl let down a cotton-reel from upstairs and banged it on my ground-floor window to disturb our loving quiet. My high tea before work consisted almost invariably of tinned salmon which I shared with Paddy, so that most days he was sick on the floor. On overcast mornings, before going on with my hopeless novel, I would take him for a walk in the nearby park where, when you touched the leaves, they left soot on the fingers. Once I took a lace worker to high tea, but she didn't sleep with me for all that. Oxford seemed more than six months away and London very far. I had fallen into a pocket out of life and out of time, but I was not unhappy.

Vivien was a Roman Catholic, but to me religion went no deeper than the sentimental hymns in the school chapel. 'Lord Dismiss us with Thy Blessing' represented the occasional mercy of God, and I enjoyed the luxurious melancholy of 'Abide with Me'. The only prize I had ever won at school was a special prize for an 'imaginative composition', given by an elderly master in memory of his son killed in the first world war. It was the first time the prize had been awarded, and being a deeply religious man he was grieved that it should go to a story about an old senile Jehovah who had been left alone in a deserted heaven.

I met the girl I was to marry after finding a note from her at the porter's lodge in Balliol protesting against my inaccuracy in writing, during the course of a film review, of the 'worship' Roman Catholics gave to the Virgin Mary, when I should have used the term 'hyperdulia'. I was interested that anyone took these subtle distinctions of an unbelievable theology seriously, and we became acquainted. Now it occurred to me, during the long empty mornings, that if I were to marry a Catholic I ought at least to learn the nature and limits of the beliefs she held. It was only fair, since she knew what I believed—in nothing supernatural. Besides, I thought, it would kill the time.

One day I took Paddy for a walk to the sooty neo-Gothic Cathedral—it possessed for me a certain gloomy power because it represented the inconceivable and the incredible. There was a wooden box for enquiries and I dropped into it a note asking for instruction. Then I went back to my high tea of tinned salmon and Paddy was sick again. I had no intention of being received into the Church. For such a thing to happen I would need to be convinced of its truth and that was not even a remote possibility.

The impossibility seemed even more pronounced a week later when I returned to the Cathedral and met Father Trollope. I was to grow fond of Trollope in the weeks which followed, but at the first sight he was all I detested most in my private image of the Church. A very tall and very fat man with big smooth jowls which looked as though they had never needed a razor, he resembled closely a character in one of those nineteenth-century paintings to be seen in art shops on the wrong side of Piccadilly—monks and cardinals enjoying their Friday abstinence by dismembering enormous lobsters and pouring great goblets of wine. Poor Trollope, his appearance maligned him. He led a very ascetic life, and one of his worst privations was the rule which, at that period, forbade him to visit the theatre, for he had been an actor in the West End—not a star, but one of those useful reliable actors who are nearly always in demand for secondary rôles. First he had become converted to Catholicism (Dr Fry, that former ogre of Berkhamsted, had persuaded his family, who lived in Lincoln under the shadow of the deanery, to oppose his conversion), and then he was driven further by some inner compulsion to the priesthood. There were many plays on his shelves among the theological books—reading them was the nearest he could get to the footlights.

It was some weeks before he told me his story, and it came like a warning hand placed on my shoulder. 'See the danger of going too far', that was the menace his story contained. 'Be very careful. Keep well within your depth. There are dangerous currents out at sea which could sweep you anywhere . . .' Father Trollope had been swept a very long way out, but the turbulent sea had not finished with him yet. He held a high position in the Catholic Nottingham world: he was Administrator of the Cathedral, well-placed to rise into a hierarchy where men of business ability are valued, but he was deeply dissatisfied with any future which could be represented as success—he hadn't yet sacrificed enough, and a few years after I left Nottingham he wrote to tell me that he was entering an Order, an Order which was to my mind the least attractive of any, the Redemptorist. What had these monks, with an obligation to dwell in all their sermons and retreats on the reality of hell, in common with this stout cheerful man who loved the smell of grease-paint and the applause at a curtain-fall? Perhaps nothing except the desire to drown. A few years later he was dead of cancer.

It was quite a while before I realized that my first impression was totally false and that I was facing the challenge of an inexplicable goodness. I would see Trollope once or twice a week for an hour's instruction, and to my own surprise I came to look forward to these occasions, so that I was disappointed when by reason of his work they were cancelled. Sometimes the place of instruction was an odd one—we began our lesson, perhaps, with a discussion on the date of the Gospels on the upper deck of a tram swaying out to some Nottingham suburb where he had business to do and concluded it with the significance of Josephus in the pious pitch-pine parlour of a convent.

I had cheated him from the first, not telling him of my motive in receiving instruction or that I was engaged to marry a Roman Catholic. At the beginning I thought that if I disclosed the truth he would consider me too easy game, and later I began to fear that he would distrust the genuineness of my conversion if it so happened that I chose to be received, for after a few weeks of serious argument the 'if' was becoming less and less improbable. Bishop Gore in his great book on religious belief wrote that his own primary difficulty was to believe in the love of God; my primary difficulty was to believe in a God at all. The date of the Gospels, the historical evidence for the existence of the man Jesus Christ: these were interesting subjects which came nowhere near the core of my disbelief. I didn't disbelieve in Christ—I disbelieved in God. If I were ever to be convinced in even the remote possibility of a supreme, omnipotent and omniscient power I realized that nothing afterwards could seem impossible. It was on the ground of a dogmatic atheism that I fought and fought hard. It was like a fight for personal survival.

My friend Antonia White many years later told me how, when she was attending the funeral of her father, an old priest, who had known her as a child, tried to persuade her to return to the Church. At last—to please him more than for any other reason—she said, 'Well then, Father, remind me

[164]

of the arguments for the existence of God.' After a long hesitation he admitted to her, 'I knew them once, but I have forgotten them.' I have suffered the same loss of memory. I can only remember that in January 1926 I became convinced of the probable existence of something we call God, though now I dislike the word with all its anthropomorphic associations and prefer Chardin's Noosphere, and my belief never came by way of those unconvincing philosophical arguments which I derided in a short story called *A Visit to Morin*.

'Oh,' it may be said, 'a young man is no match for a trained priest,' but in fact, at twenty-two, fresh from Oxford and its intellectual exercises, I was more capable of arguing an abstract issue or debating an historical point than I am today. The experience of a long life may possibly increase one's intuition of human character, but the mass of memories and associations which we drag around with us like an over-full suitcase on our interminable journey would weary me now at the start with all such arguments as we indulged in then. I cannot be bothered to remember—I accept. With the approach of death I care less and less about religious truth. One hasn't long to wait for revelation or darkness.

Although I was not received till early February 1926, I must have made my decision some weeks before, for I wrote flippantly to my mother in January, in the course of a letter full of other concerns, 'I expect you have guessed that I am embracing the Scarlet Woman.' The flippancy was fictitious: the fun of the intellectual exercise was over. I had reached the limit of the land and there the sea waited, if I didn't turn back. I was laughing to keep my courage up.

The first General Confession, which precedes conditional baptism and which covers the whole of a man's previous life, is a humiliating ordeal. Later we may become hardened to the formulas of confession and sceptical about ourselves: we may only half intend to keep the promises we make, until continual failure or the circumstances of our private life, finally make it impossible to make any promises at all and many of us abandon Confession and Communion to join the Foreign Legion of the Church and fight for a city of which we are no longer full citizens. But in the first Confession a convert really believes in his own promises. I carried mine down with me like heavy stones into an empty corner of the Cathedral, dark already in the early afternoon, and the only witness of my baptism was a woman who had been dusting the chairs. I took the name of Thomas—after St Thomas the doubter and not Thomas Aquinas—and then I went on to the *Nottingham Journal* office and the football results and the evening of potato chips.

I remember very clearly the nature of my emotion as I walked away from the Cathedral: there was no joy in it at all, only a sombre apprehension. I had made the first move with a view to my future marriage, but now the land had given way under my feet and I was afraid of where the tide would take me. Even my marriage seemed uncertain to me now. Suppose I discovered in myself what Father Trollope had once discovered, the desire to be a priest . . . At that moment it seemed by no means impossible. Only now after

[166]

more than forty years I am able to smile at the unreality of
my fear and feel at the same time a sad nostalgia for it, since
I lost more than I gained when the fear belonged irrevocably
to the past.

Chapter 10

I

I was earning nothing and learning very little on the *Journal*, and I had begun again to draw an allowance from my father who could ill afford it. I decided, between one high tea of tinned salmon and another, to leave Nottingham and try once more to find a job in London. I thought I was leaving Nottingham without regret, and I would have disbelieved anyone who had told me then that the city was embedded unforgettably in my imagination, and that the memory of it would stay with me over the next forty years like a photograph of a woman which one preserves in a drawer one doesn't know why, even when the relationship has seemed a long time dead.

Ten years passed before I wrote in a book called *A Gun for Sale* a description of my first morning in the city.

'There was no dawn that day in Nottwich. Fog lay over the city like a night sky with no stars. The air in the streets was clear. You had only to imagine that it was night. The first tram crawled out of its shed and took the steel track down towards the market. An old piece of newspaper blew up against the door of the Royal Theatre and flattened out. In the streets on the outskirts of Nottwich an old man plodded by with a pole tapping at the windows. The stationer's win-

dow in the High Street was full of prayer books and bibles:
a printed card remained among them, a relic of armistice
day, like the old drab wreath of Haig poppies by the war
memorial: "Look up, and swear by the slain of the war that
you'll never forget".'

The card, with its quotation from Siegfried Sassoon, had
been in the window when I arrived in Nottingham in
November and it was still there when I left in February.

In 1945, when the second war was over, I began to plan a
novel set in Nottingham, and I revisited the city on the
excuse of refreshing my memory, though it wasn't a 'necessary' journey, the only kind which in those days we were
expected to make. I found the essentials were still the same,
though the 'boots' had disappeared from the Black Dog Inn.
I wrote no more than the first chapter of the novel before I
turned instead to *The Heart of the Matter*, but in 1957 I
adapted the idea into an unsatisfactory play, *The Potting
Shed*, in which I gave an off-stage part to my unsatisfactory
dog. Our walks together along the River Trent and down to
the goose-market forced their way into the play, and 'My
landlady has a penchant for tinned salmon,' I remarked
through a character's mouth. 'My dog likes it, but it often
makes him sick. He's not a very good dog—parents unknown.' No, whatever Tynan might think, Paddy was never
intended to be God. He was just himself.

I was to continue my effort to write romantic novels for
some years to come, but when I finally realized their futility,
it was to my memory of the solitary months in Nottingham
that I returned for help; there I found a different subject.

The furnished room in All Saints Terrace drew me back, like the Common at Berkhamsted, the abandoned trenches, and I made it the home of a libidinous clergyman who, unlike my grandfather, had been unfrocked against his will.

Time since I left Oxford had moved as slowly as the unemployed bands of those days, shifting, with hands spread out, along a pavement edge: the British-American Tobacco Company, the tutoring in the Pennines, the long evening hours on the *Journal* with little to do, the five hundred words a day on a novel which I was half aware belonged to the past and would never be published. Suddenly the hands of the clock swung round as though a hand were correcting the hour. I left Nottingham at the end of January, and in the first week of March I had been accepted on trial as a subeditor by *The Times*.

2

I was happy on *The Times*, and I could have remained happy there for a lifetime, if I had not in the end succeeded in publishing a novel, but not the one I was about to finish when I left Nottingham. My regular hours were from four in the afternoon to eleven at night, though occasionally I was forced to stay later. But more often, while my services remained as little valuable as they had been at Nottingham, I would be sent away before my time, and this worried me. It seemed to me only too likely that I would not survive the period of trial, but finally the leisurely life of the home subeditors (there must have been about ten of us) calmed my nerves and I began to realize I was as safe as though I had entered the Civil Service. No one on *The Times* was ever known to be sacked or to resign. I remember with pleasure —it was a symbol of the peaceful life—the slow burning fire in the subeditors' room, the gentle thud of coals as they dropped one by one in the old black grate.

Ivy House, All Saints Terrace, and my sour widow had been exchanged for a bed-sitting-room in Battersea and a far from melancholy landlady. She was untidy, exuberant and absent-minded. Articles of furniture regularly disappeared from my room towards the end of a month to reappear a week later; she had put them in hock to overcome a temporary difficulty. When I went out in the evening to Battersea Station to catch a train to Blackfriars I would pass an imposing building with a notice hanging on the railings: 'It is forbidden to throw stones at the Polytechnic'. Wandering along those streets I was passing unconsciously through the scenery of a future book, *It's a Battlefield*.

My five pounds a week was quite adequate to keep a single man. I was charged, I think, thirty shillings a week for my room and breakfast, and my dinner in *The Times* canteen seldom cost me more than elevenpence—for elevenpence I got two kippers, a pot of tea, and a slice of syrup roll.

Paddy I could no longer retain. I left him at Berkhamsted without regret. Luckily he had wormed his way into my mother's affection. He was the first dog she had ever cared for—perhaps because like a difficult child he was both nervous and independent. He never quite recovered his

[171]

mental equilibrium after a picture in the drawing-room fell down beside him, and in those days there was no psycho-analyst for dogs.

I had been on *The Times* only two months when the General Strike was declared. *The Times* was the only paper which continued to be issued without interruption from the first day of the strike, although at the beginning it appeared in the form of a single multigraphed sheet. Our success aroused the jealousy of Winston Churchill, who seized a quarter of our paper stocks for his extravagant *London Gazette*. As the *Gazette* was badly edited, over-printed and maldistributed, great bundles of his journal, manufactured with our paper, were dumped loose around the streets for anyone to pick up. Being one of the editorial staff I was automatically a strike-breaker, and there were moments of drama, even in the quiet of Printing House Square.

Among the notices on the wall of every room there had always hung instructions on what to do in case of fire—if a bell rang three times we were to file out in an orderly way and proceed I forget where. It was an instruction which seemed as far removed from reality as the little book on style with which each of us was supplied, and in which we read that we must not spell 'bunkum' 'buncombe' or 'Marquess' 'Marquis'. Now, when an unmistakable fire-alarm sounded in the afternoon on the second day of the strike, no one paid any attention. We were all of us a little sleepy, for we had been up the whole previous night while the multigraph machines turned out the famous single sheet of May 5, 1926, Number 44263 of *The Times*, price twopence. We had worked as loaders and packers, for there was little subediting to do, even though the single sheet finally managed to include, apart from news of the strike, a weather report, broadcasting, sport, Stock Exchange, and a Court Page of five lines which might have been written by Sir John Betjeman ('The Prince of Wales returned to London from Biarritz last night, travelling from Paris by air'). The machines did not stop till eight in the morning, and then we had all walked home, for there were no trams, no tubes, no buses. Little wonder that not one of us paid any attention at first to the fire-alarm.

The bell rang once, twice, three times. Someone asked with mild curiosity, 'A fire?' After a while the assistant chief subeditor, Colonel Maude, rose and moved with his usual elegant and leisurely gait into the corridor. He was a man of great courtesy, very tall and slim with a soft blond moustache; you would have taken him for a military attaché but never for a journalist. I remember that he always apologized to me in a low drawling voice when he handed me any work at all—even a small paragraph for the News in Brief on a prize vegetable marrow—and now, when he returned to the room and sat down, it took quite a time to realize that *The Times*—so he was telling us—had been set on fire. He was seated again at the long table, which was usually presided over by the chief subeditor, George Anderson, but it was opening-time and at opening-time Anderson always took a short leave of absence. The strikers apparently had squirted petrol through a grating into the basement and had managed to set alight one of the great rolls of paper which stood there.

Maude obviously was not disturbed, there was no copy to deal with, and my fellow subeditors chatted a little while on the subject of fires in general and the feasibility of burning down *The Times*. One of the subeditors was an elderly man who ran a small farm in the country and therefore always dealt with the agricultural page. He told us a few anecdotes about rick-fires, which passed the time until the all-clear sounded. Later that night there was a small fight between the loaders, of whom I was one, and the pickets in Printing House Square; the Sporting Department acted as storm-troops and there were few casualties. Nor was there any bad feeling. The revolutionary atmosphere south of the river died away on the bridges.

More from curiosity than from any wish to support the Establishment I became a special constable and I used to parade of a morning with a genuine policeman the length of Vauxhall Bridge. There was a wonderful absence of traffic, it was a beautiful hushed London that we were not to know again until the blitz, and there was the exciting sense of living on a frontier, close to violence. Armoured cars paraded the streets, and just as during the blitz certain areas, Bloomsbury and Euston among them, were more unhealthy than others like Hampstead and St John's Wood, so Camberwell and Hammersmith were now considered more dangerous than the City. Our two-man patrol always ceased at the south end of Vauxhall Bridge, for beyond lay the enemy streets where groups of strikers stood outside the public houses. A few years later my sympathies would have lain with them, but the great depression was still some years away: the middle-class had not yet been educated by the hunger-marchers. On the side of the Establishment it was a game, a break in the monotony of earning a secure living, at its most violent the atmosphere was that of a rugger match played against a team from a rather rough council school which didn't stick to the conventional rules. 'I'm almost sorry now that it's over,' I wrote home, 'as we had as much free beer as we wanted at the office while it was on.'

There was yet another advantage. I felt accepted now. I even received a silver match-box from the management. My three months' trial was not yet finished, but in the camaraderie of free beer and unusual duties I had become an established member of the staff. Oxford had at least taught me to drink pint by pint with any man.

Of my companions in the subeditors' room (most of them seemed much older than I was) I remember faces and characteristics more than names. The youngest subeditor, apart from myself, was so fastidious that he could eat nothing, he said, which had been touched by the human hand: for dinner in the canteen he took only a cup of tea. Yet he was plump enough, so that he must have had somewhere at home a hygienic source of supply. I would try to tempt him with a tin of sardines, but there was obviously some doubt in his mind as to what happened between the netting of the fish and the tinning. I connected his fastidiousness with his employment, for he was in charge of the Court Page and he had a desk all to himself, loaded with such superior reference books as the *Almanach de Gotha*, Debrett's *Peerage* and Burke's *Landed Gentry*.

There were other faces which returned to me often later in dreams. At least once a year, until quite recently, I dreamt I was entering the subeditors' room after a long absence. I would find an empty chair but not in my old place, and I would feel a sense of shame because I had been away so long and had returned only temporarily (the faces I saw around me were many of them by this time the faces of the dead). I would take Crockford down from the shelf over the coal-grate and check the name of an obscure vicar who had grown a prize vegetable marrow.

3

I can think of no better career for a young novelist than to be for some years a subeditor on a rather conservative newspaper. The hours, from four till around midnight, give him plenty of time to do his own work in the morning when he is still fresh from sleep—let the office employ him during his hours of fatigue. He has the company of intelligent and agreeable men of greater experience than his own: he is not enclosed by himself in a small room tormented by the problems of expression; and, except for rare periods of rush, even his working hours leave him time for books and conversation (most of us brought a book to read between one piece of copy and another). Nor is the work monotonous. Rather as in the game of Scrabble the same letters are continually producing different words; no one knows at four o'clock what the evening may produce, and death does not keep a conventional hour.

The young subeditor gains too some small insights into the vanities of the famous. J. M. Barrie before making a speech would send to *The Times* a typescript which included some passages that his audience must have taken for whimsical impromptus. (His speeches were always printed verbatim in the first person—a distinction he shared only with the Prime Minister.) 'I see the Archbishop of Canterbury smiling sceptically in my direction and wickedly shaking his head . . .' I would read this at four-thirty in an after-dinner speech which was to be delivered at ten. Did the Archbishop have a prompt copy?

Another amusement was to discover unconscious obscenities in the copy handed in—not always perhaps unconscious. Charles Marriott, the art critic, was continually trying, or so it seemed, to slip something by, and the correspondence editor himself was responsible, at the time when Hyde Park was much in the news because of the Chiozza Money case, for the headline, 'Blocking in Hyde Park'.

And while the young writer is spending these amusing and unexacting hours, he is learning lessons valuable to his own craft. He is removing the clichés of reporters; he is compressing a story to the minimum length possible without ruining its effect. A writer with a sprawling style is unlikely to emerge from such an apprenticeship. It is the opposite training to the penny-a-liner.

The man who was of chief importance to me in those days

was the chief subeditor, George Anderson. I hated him in my first week, but I grew almost to love him before three years had passed. A small elderly Scotsman with a flushed face and a laconic humour,* he drove a new subeditor hard with his sarcasm. Sometimes I almost fancied myself back at school again, and I was always glad when five-thirty came, for immediately the clock marked the hour when the pubs opened he would take his bowler hat from the coat-rack and disappear for thirty minutes to his favourite bar. His place would be taken by the gentle and courteous Colonel Maude. Maude was careful to see that the new recruit was given no story which could possibly stretch his powers, and if he had been chief subeditor I doubt if I would ever have got further than a News in Brief paragraph. At the stroke of six, when Anderson returned and hung up his bowler, his face would have turned a deeper shade of red, to match the rose he carried always in his buttonhole, and his shafts of criticism, as he scanned my copy with perhaps a too flagrant headline, would have acquired a tang of friendliness. More than two years went by, and my novel *The Man Within* had been accepted by a publisher, before I discovered one slack evening, when there was hardly enough news to fill the Home pages for the ten o'clock edition, that a poet *manqué* had dug those defences of disappointed sarcasm. When a

* I am grateful to Mr Arthur Crook, the editor of *The Times Literary Supplement*, for this characteristic example. 'E. Colston Shepherd, the former aeronautical correspondent of *The Times*, once told me that he was infuriated by a very truncated version of a story he had written with great care. He complained bitterly to Anderson, saying that his story had been very badly cut. "Heavily, my dear Shep, heavily. Not badly. I cut it myself."'

young man, Anderson had published a volume of trans-
lations from Verlaine; he had sent it to Swinburne at The
Pines and he had been entertained there for tea and kind
words by Watts-Dunton, though I don't think he was
allowed to see the poet. He never referred to the episode
again, but I began to detect in him a harsh but paternal apprehension for another young man, flushed with pride in a
first book, who might suffer the same disappointment. When
I came to resign he spent a long time arguing with me, and I
think his real reason for trying to prevent my departure was
that he foresaw a time might come when novel-writing
would fail me and I would need, like himself, a quiet and
secure life with the pubs opening at half-past five and the
coal settling in the grate.

No other group of men—not even the air-raid wardens at
my post in Gower Street during the blitz nor my fellows
later in the Secret Service—have so planted themselves,
nameless though they may have become, in my memory.
Perhaps this is always the case with a young man's first real
job: the impression in the wax will never go quite so deep
again. Even those with whom I had only a transient contact
are impressed there, Geoffrey Dawson, the editor (whatever
his later politics of appeasement I can only remember his
kindness to a young employee), Vladimir Poliakoff, the
diplomatic correspondent, in a grey homburg hat with a
very large brim, who would come into our room to consult
the files, carrying with him an air of worldliness and mystery
(why was he not reading them next door in the foreign room
where he naturally belonged? Perhaps he wished to remain

[179]

for obscure reasons of state incognito), the medical corre-spondent, Doctor McNair Wilson, who was, I think, more an authority on Napoleon than on medicine, and in my last year the future editor, Barrington-Ward, a cold complacent man, prematurely bald, who suddenly appeared, like an un-spoken threat, unexplained and inexplicable, in the room of kindly old Murray Brumwell, the assistant editor. He had, I can see now, the smooth assured air of a Dauphin, but I thought of him even in those early days as Pecksniff, though Pecksniff had a good head of hair. Later, when I had fallen on evil days and tried to return to *The Times*, he wrote me a letter which Pecksniff could not have bettered. 'Since your day,' he wrote with a vague reminiscence of Longfellow, 'the tents have been folded and moved on.'

4

That summer I finished my second novel and wrote to my mother, 'The gamble of the thing is getting it typewritten, as one has to have two copies against wear and tear. Could you advance me five pounds and let me pay you back at the rate of about ten shillings a week?' They were five wasted pounds, and I can only hope I paid her back. I sent the type-script to Heinemann. It was July, 1926. There was an acknowledgement and afterwards a long silence—it seemed as irrevocably lost as though I had dropped it into the coal-fire of the subeditors' room. Months went by . . . the new year came . . . February . . . March . . . I even began a third book which I soon abandoned, a detective novel, the first of so many unfinished novels—*Fanatic Arabia*, which in spite of its title taken from Doughty began in a London bus station and was never intended to move further than the Midlands; *Across the Border*, an African story, which opened in Berkhamsted; a school novel of a timid boy's blackmail of the housemaster who had protected him; a spy story called *A Sense of Security* . . . Even today, until I have passed a quarter of the course, I am uncertain whether I will be able to reach the end.

The detective story I still believe to have been ingenious. A young governess was found murdered in a country house, and a multiplicity of strange clues baffled the police. Only the local priest recognized behind them a child's psychology and realized where they led—to a small girl of twelve who had committed the crime because her beloved governess was in love with a man. The priest, of course, did not betray the child . . . Now I can detect the various threads of my short experience which intermingled: my sister's governess, jealousy of the man she was to marry, perhaps the long summers at Harston House, even Father Trollope and my new conversion; yet, if I had been asked about the story then, I would have said it bore no relation whatever to my life.

It is better to remain in ignorance of oneself and to forget easily. Let the unemployed continue to lurk around the pubs in Vauxhall Bridge Road and the kidnappers drive out of Heidelberg towards the frontier, safely and completely forgotten; we ought to leave the forgotten to the night. If one day they find their way into a book, it should be without our connivance and so disguised that we don't recognize them when we see them again. All that we can easily recognize as our experience in a novel is mere reporting: it has a place, but an unimportant one. It provides an anecdote, it fills in gaps in the narrative. It may legitimately provide a background, and sometimes we have to fall back on it when the imagination falters. Perhaps a novelist has a greater ability to forget than other men—he has to forget or become sterile. What he forgets is the compost of the imagination.

5

Eight months went by with no reply from Heinemann, and at last I wrote to remind them of my typescript. I felt sure that this would bring me no luck, and I was not surprised when a bulky package came quickly back. The managing director, Charles Evans, wrote himself, apologizing for the delay. There had been two contradictory reports, so he had wished to read the novel himself and now, in spite of his interest, he regretted ... At the same time he hoped I would show him my next book. That this was a polite formula for a mislaid manuscript seems obvious to me now, but I was a novice and I was so encouraged by his words that I never sent the manuscript elsewhere, content to abide by Heinemann's decision. I would write one novel more, I decided, and, if the third book proved as unsuccessful as the others, I would abandon this ambition forever. I was established on *The Times*, and marriage would be possible in another year.

I knew nothing of a letter lying in my parents' files, like a little time-bomb, which was to make that future seem doubtful. Perhaps they had forgotten it themselves, as one forgets an unpleasant fact one has lived with for a long time and cannot alter, and it was only my sudden illness which brought it back to mind.

The doctor to whom I complained of recurrent pains was a dangerous man to consult. I had picked him at random as I wandered down a Battersea Street troubled by a sharper stab of pain than usual. His brass plate caught my eye on a house not far from the railway viaduct. Smoke coated his panes, an aspidistra drooped on his window-sill, starved of tea-leaves, and his door vibrated gently as the trains emerged from Clapham Junction. The doctor opened the door himself, a young Hindu, and showed me into a dingy consulting room where he must have been waiting with eastern patience for the sick to seek him out. He judged my pulse and took my temperature and prodded where the pain lay; then he gave me a bottle of medicine ready prepared which he said would do the trick. I think he charged six shillings for the consultation and the bottle. Luckily over the telephone I told my brother, who was now an intern at Westminster Hospital, what had happened, and that night I found myself in a public ward at his hospital to be operated on for appendicitis with the least possible delay. The Hindu doctor stayed in my mind—a symbol of the shabby, the inefficient and possibly the illegal, and he left his trace, with another doctor, on some pages of *A Gun for Sale*.

As I lay in the ward after the operation (in those days they kept the patient at least a week) I began to plan my third novel, the forlorn hope. I called it *The Man Within*, and it began with a hunted man, who was to appear again and again in later less romantic books. But curiously enough there came to me also in the ward, with the death of a patient, the end of a book which I would not begin to write for another six years.

It was our second death. The first we had barely noticed: an old man dying from cancer of the mouth. He had been too old and ill to join in the high jinks of the ward, the courtship of nurses, the teasings, the ticklings and the pinches. When the screens went up around his bed the silence in his corner was no deeper than it had always been. But the second death disturbed the whole ward. The first was inevitable fate, the second was contingency.

The victim was a boy of ten. He had been brought into the ward one afternoon, having broken his leg at football. He was a cheerful child with a rosy face and his parents stayed and chatted with him for a while until he settled down to sleep. One of the nurses ten minutes later paused by his bed and leant over him. Suddenly there was a burst of activity, a doctor came hurrying in, screens went up around the bed, an oxygen machine was run squeaking across the floor, but the child had outdistanced them all to death. By the time the parents reached home, a message was waiting to summon them urgently back. They came and sat beside the bed, and to shut out the sound of the mother's tears and cries all my companions in the ward lay with their ear-phones on, listening—there was nothing else for them to hear—to Children's Hour. All my companions but not myself. There is a splinter of ice in the heart of a writer. I watched and listened. This was something which one day I might need: the woman speaking, uttering the banalities she must have remembered from some woman's magazine, a genuine grief that could communicate only in clichés. 'My boy, my boy, why did you not wait till I came?' The father sat silent with his hat on his knees, and you could tell that even in his unhappiness he was embarrassed by the banality of his wife's words, by the scene she was so badly playing to the public ward, and he wanted desperately to get away home and be alone. 'Human language,' Flaubert wrote, 'is like a cracked kettle on which we beat out tunes for bears to dance to, when all the time we are longing to move the stars to pity.'

After two weeks I returned to *The Times*, but perhaps because I had returned too soon, I fainted my first evening at work. I was given another week's holiday and went to Brighton, as I had so often gone in the past with my aunt after a childish sickness. I thought no more of the affair, unaware of the time-bomb ticking in my mother's desk. (I have the little machine before me now, a letter written five years before, in 1921, to my father by Kenneth Richmond.)

My mother wrote to me in Brighton asking me when I returned to London to go and see my old analyst. I was a little puzzled, but I was pleased at the thought of seeing him again; I was aware that he had deliberately severed our relationship, for fear that I might come to depend on him, but to me he represented the happiest period of my life. One night at Brighton I was sitting quite alone, or so I thought, in one of the shelters on the front, when a voice spoke to me unexpectedly in the darkness. 'Good evening,' it said in the accent of old age.

'Good evening,' I replied, trying to see through the night.

'I am Old Moore,' the voice said. So perhaps I should have been warned.

Kenneth Richmond no longer lived in the trim little house in Devonshire Terrace off Lancaster Gate, but a larger and darker house without any memories for me. We talked a little of my second novel and he offered to help me in my search for a publisher, but I felt sure this was not the purpose of my invitation. And then, speaking as unexpectedly as Old Moore on the Brighton front, he reminded me of what I had quite forgotten, the occasion when I had once fainted at his dinner table. Afterwards he had taken me to see a specialist in Harley Street: a small dark intense man whose features are now confused in my memory with those of the actor Ernest Milton and of Colonel de Castries of Dien Bien Phu.

'Your mother tells me you are engaged to be married,' Richmond said. 'Now about this fainting attack at *The Times . . .*'

I remembered how the specialist had questioned me about earlier attacks of fainting in the summer stuffiness of the school chapel. Many children, I told myself, went through such a phase.

'Doctor Riddick diagnosed epilepsy,' Richmond said.

Epilepsy, cancer and leprosy—these are the three medical terms which rouse the greatest fear in the untutored, and at twenty-two one is unprepared for so final a judgment. Epilepsy, Richmond went on, could be inherited: I must consider the risk carefully before marriage, and he sought to comfort me by pointing out that Dostoievsky too had suffered from epilepsy. I couldn't think of a reply. Dostoievsky was a dead Victorian writer, not a youth without a book to his name who had pledged himself to marry . . . 'Let me see your novel,' Richmond said, meaning to be kind. 'What is the title?'

'*The Episode*,' I said.

I left the house and began walking fast towards South Kensington, the King's Road, Oakley Street, the Albert Bridge, away from *this* episode. When I got home I wrote a letter; they had left things rather late, I said, before informing me. Poor souls, I can sympathize with them now as I read the letters which were written to them on the same day by Richmond and Doctor Riddick. Doctor Riddick's was frightening, even in its moderation. 'The attacks to which he is occasionally subject are, I think, epileptic; but since he has lost consciousness in three only, there is a reasonably good chance that, with suitable treatment, the condition may be arrested.' The treatment seemed to consist of good walks and Keppler's Malt Extract. Richmond's letter was more encouraging, and my mother in pencil has pathetically underlined all the optimistic phrases she could find, perhaps to comfort my father—'quite likely to clear up completely' ... 'no cause for alarm'—even the phrase about Dostoievsky is trotted out and surprisingly underlined, but then follows what I think was unfair and dangerous advice: 'We agreed that Graham ought not to be told what is the matter in any terms that included the word epilepsy.'

Was the diagnosis right? With the hindsight of forty years, free from any recurrence, I don't believe it, but I believed it then. I remember next day standing on an Underground platform and trying to summon the will and the courage to jump. It was not my new Catholicism which restrained me. There was no theological despair in what I felt. I was simply tired out by the thought of starting a completely different future than the one I had planned. But suicide requires greater courage than Russian roulette, the trains came and went, and soon I took the moving staircase to the upper world.

My next thought was of an elderly priest, Father Talbot, of the Oratory. I had been passed on to him—a fashion priests have—by Trollope, and I had spent many agreeable hours with him in discussion and argument at his quiet chambers in the Oratory, as unclerical as rooms in college. He was a man of very liberal views, and surely, I thought despairingly, he would have some answer to my greatest problem: that if I were epileptic, I must avoid having children. Surely there must be some cranny of canon law or moral theology that would contain a ruling for just such a case as mine.

He asked me to go out with him, and for the next hour we drove in a taxi, crossing and recrossing the same rectangle between the Brompton Road and Bayswater, just as we crossed and recrossed the same lines of argument. Under no circumstances at all was contraception permissible. 'The Church forbids me to marry then?'

'Of course we don't forbid marriage.'

'Do you expect married people to live together without making love?'

'The Church expects you to trust God, that's all.'

Up and down, over and over, a useless embroidery which made no pattern.

How differently he would have answered my question today, telling me, I have no doubt, to follow my conscience, which even then was elastic enough for almost anything. Catholics have sometimes accused me of making my clerical characters, Father Rank in *The Heart of the Matter* and Father James in *The Living Room*, fail unnecessarily before the human problems they were made to face. 'A real priest,' I have been told, 'would have had something further to say, he would have shown a deeper comprehension, he wouldn't have left the situation so unchanged.' But that is exactly what in those days, before John Roncalli was elected Pope, the priesthood was compelled to do. There was no failure in comprehension. Father Talbot was a man of the greatest human sympathy, but he had no solution for me at all. There was only one hard answer he could honestly give ('the Church knows all the rules,' as Father Rank said), while the meter of the taxi ticked away the repetitions of our fruitless argument. It was the Rock of Peter I was aware of in our long drive, and though it repulsed me, I couldn't help admiring its unyielding façade.

My misery did not last long. My brother, by this time a doctor, was the first to question the diagnosis, and then the medical correspondent, Doctor McNair Wilson, who had been in the subeditors' room when I fainted, confirmed that he had seen no symptom whatever of epilepsy.

6

I married, and I was happy. In the evenings I worked at *The Times*, in the mornings I worked on my third novel. Now when I write I put down on the page a mere skeleton of a novel—nearly all my revisions are in the nature of additions, of second thoughts to make the bare bones live— but in those days to revise was to prune and prune and prune. I was much tempted, perhaps because of my admiration for the Metaphysical poets, by exaggerated similes and my wife became an adept at shooting them down. There was one, I remember, comparing something or someone in the quiet landscape of Sussex to a leopard crouching in a tree, which gave a name to the whole species. Leopards would be marked daily on the manuscript, but it took a great many years for me to get the beasts under control, and they growl at me sometimes yet.

One day in the winter of 1928 I lay in bed with a bad attack of flu, listening to my wife in the kitchen washing up the breakfast things. I had posted copies of the typescript to

Heinemann and The Bodley Head about ten days before, and I was now resigned to a long delay. Hadn't I waited last time nine months for a refusal? Anyway, uncertainty was more agreeable to live with than the confirmation of failure. The telephone rang in the sitting-room and my wife came in and told me, 'There's a Mr Evans wants to speak to you.'

'I don't know anyone called Evans,' I said. 'Tell him I'm in bed. Tell him I'm ill.' Suddenly a memory came back to me: Evans was the chairman of Heinemann's, and I ran to snatch the telephone.

'I've read your novel,' he said. 'We'd like to publish it. Would it be possible for you to look in here at eleven?' My flu was gone in that moment and never returned.

Nothing in a novelist's life later can equal that moment— the acceptance of his first book. Triumph is unalloyed by any doubt of the future. Mounting the wide staircase in the elegant eighteenth-century house in Great Russell Street I could have no foreboding of the failures and frustrations of the next ten years.

Charles Evans was a remarkable publisher. With his bald head and skinny form he looked like a family solicitor lean with anxieties, but a solicitor who had taken an overdose of some invigorating vitamin. His hands and legs were never still. He did everything, from shaking hands to ringing a bell, in quick jerks. Perhaps because the flu had not entirely departed, I expected at any moment the legendary figures of Heinemann authors to enter the room behind me, Mr Galsworthy, Mr John Masefield, Mr Maugham, Mr George Moore, Mr Joseph Hergesheimer. I sat on the edge of the chair ready to leap up. The bearded ghost of Conrad rumbled on the rooftops with the rain.

I was quite prepared to hear what I had always understood to be the invariable formula—'of course a first novel is a great risk, we shall have to begin with a small royalty'—but that was not Evans's way with a young author. Just as he had substituted the direct telephone call for the guarded letter, so now he brushed aside any ancient rite of initiation.

'No publisher,' he said, 'can ever guarantee success, but all the same we have hopes . . .' The royalty would begin at $12\frac{1}{2}$ per cent, with a fifty-pound advance, he recommended me to take an agent, for in the future there might be subsidiary rights to deal with . . . I went out dazed into Great Russell Street. My day-dream had never continued further than a promise of publication and now my publisher (proud phrase, 'my publisher') was suggesting even the possibility of success.

He was as good as his word, selling more than 8,000 copies of the novel, so that I was all the more unprepared for the failures which succeeded it. In the flush of that success I would have refused to believe that success is slow and not sudden and that ten years later, with my tenth novel, *The Power and the Glory*, the publisher could risk printing only 3,500 copies, one thousand copies more than he had printed of my first novel.

The Man Within is very young and very sentimental. It has no meaning for me today and I can see no reason for its success. It is like the book of a complete stranger, of a kind for which I have never much cared—and this makes another judgment on the book yet more mysterious to me. My uncle Eppy—the rich worldly business uncle of the Brazilian Warrant Agency—wrote to me: 'It could only have been written by a Greene.' I thought of my parents, I thought of all those aunts and uncles and cousins who had gathered together at Christmas, and of the two unknown Greene grandfathers, the guilt-ridden clergyman and the melancholic sugar-planter dead of yellow fever in St Kitts, and then I thought of the novel, the story of a hunted man, of smuggling and treachery, of murder and suicide, and I wondered what on earth he was driving at. I wonder still.

<h1 style="text-align:center">7</h1>

Leaving *The Times* was even more difficult than joining it and took almost as long. A few months after the publication of *The Man Within*, while I struggled with another novel, *The Name of Action* (the only good thing about the book was its title and that was suggested to me by Clemence Dane), I wrote to Charles Evans a blackmailing letter: I told him I must choose between *The Times* and novel-writing—I couldn't continue to do both. He replied offering me, if I chose to resign, six hundred pounds a year for three years (half to be supplied by my American publisher) in return for three novels. I did so choose, but how was I to set about it? I had been happy on *The Times*, I couldn't just write a letter to the manager and walk out. I consulted George Anderson, and we held long dialogues together, while he reasoned with me. I had a great future, he assured me—one day, if I were only patient for a few more years, I might hope to be the correspondence editor. Already, when the correspondence editor was on holiday, I tasted the glory of deputizing for him and this brought me into direct contact with the editor, Geoffrey Dawson himself. Closeted with the editor every afternoon at four o'clock I argued the merits of the letters and we decided which was to lead the page. I was exalted by the contact, especially when, as sometimes happened, I won the argument and even perhaps secured the promotion of one of Walter Sickert's frequent letters which offended Dawson's tidy mind by being almost illegibly written over large sheets of lined paper in thick black ink, apparently with a matchstick and usually with an impenetrable smudge over an operative word, a calligraphy which suited his savage *non sequiturs* on subjects far removed from painting.

At last Anderson realized how strong was my determination to leave, but he agreed that first I must have a word with the editor, and the editor was hopelessly elusive. There were even moments when I wondered whether Anderson had warned him of my intention. If I tried to make an appointment he was heavily engaged, if I went to his room it was empty or he was busy with a distinguished visitor. It was weeks before I caught him—I had the uncomfortable sense of doing something beyond the bounds of polite manners like wearing a bright coloured tie with a dinner jacket. Indeed I began to believe that no subeditor had ever before resigned from *The Times*, just as no one had ever been sacked from the paper since the ungentlemanly days of Lord

Northcliffe. Dawson, when I cornered him at last, took the conversation urbanely into his own hands. He said he understood that I had written a novel, and he congratulated me on its success—his wife had demanded a copy from her circulating library. *The Times*, he assured me, would have no objection if I continued to write novels in my spare time. The art critic, Mr Charles Marriott, had done so for many years, and even the dramatic critic, Mr Charles Morgan, had published one or two. Indeed the time might have almost come to try me out with an occasional third leader. However, if my mind were really made up, he could only say it was a rash and unfortunate decision.

I had a further interview before leaving on December 31st 1929, with the assistant editor, Murray Brumwell, who resembled an elderly schoolmaster and perhaps for that reason always transformed me into a tongue-tied pupil. It was too late to argue with me now, he said, but he would implore me to take care of my health and not to overwork. I smiled a little, thinking how I had been doing two jobs and working eleven hours a day. It was only later I realized that overwork is not a matter of hours and that he had good reason.

So I left the coal-grate and the faces under the green eye-shields, faces which remain as vivid to me now when the names of their owners are forgotten as those of close friends and women I have loved. In the years to come I was bitterly to regret my decision. I left *The Times* the author of a successful first novel. I thought I was a writer already and that the world was at my feet, but life wasn't like that. It was only a false start.

Chapter 11

I

The conditions of writing change absolutely between the first novel and the second: the first is an adventure, the second is a duty. The first is like a sprint which leaves you exhausted and triumphant beside the track. With the second the writer has been transformed into a long-distance runner —the finishing tape is out of sight, at the end of life. He must guard his energies and plan ahead. A long endurance is more exhausting than a sprint, and less heroic. One may sometimes envy Radiguet and Alain-Fournier whom death forestalled before they embarked on the long cross-country run.

The Man Within was, it is true, the third novel I had completed, but the first two had been clumsy exercises. I had been in training only, and there still remained other possibilities—British-American Tobacco or the Lancashire General Insurance Company. With all its faults of sentimentality and over-writing *The Man Within* was professional. I found myself committed to the long-distance race.

I sometimes find myself wishing that, before starting the second novel, *The Name of Action*, I had found an experi-

enced mentor. If Robert Louis Stevenson had been alive*
he would have been only ten years older than I am now, and
perhaps I would have found the courage to consult him in
distant Samoa and have sent him my first book. He had
always seemed to me 'one of the family'. I had lived as a boy
on the fringes of his world: his relative and biographer,
Graham Balfour, had come to our house, my beautiful aunt
would often arrive from a stay with his friend Sidney Colvin
and his wife, the former Mrs Sitwell, whom as a young man
Stevenson had loved and whom he had met in the house of
my great-aunt Maud of Number 11. Names which appeared
in his Collected Letters were photographs in our family
album. In the nursery we played on the bagatelle board
which had belonged to him. Surely from my relative in
Samoa I might have received better and more astringent
counsel than from my publisher, Charles Evans, who was
determined to shut his eyes to the disastrous failings of his
young discovery. I even received an enthusiastic telegram
from Evans welcoming the typescript of the second novel—
how could I tell how bad it really was? Evans must have
known, but he was determined to keep it dark for the time.
He had a reputation for discovering young writers, and he
couldn't admit a mistake too quickly.

I don't think I ever really believed in the book in spite of
the telegram. I know I despaired of it often, as I plodded
with my unlikely hero through the streets of Trier, on my

* It is seldom realized how short was Stevenson's career: he began
his first attempt at a novel (and abandoned it) when he was twenty-
five, and he died at forty-four.

last holiday before I left *The Times*. In most of my novels I can remember passages, even chapters, which gave me at the time I wrote them a sense of satisfaction—'this at least has come off'. So I felt, however mistakenly, with the trial scene in *The Man Within*, and later with Querry's voyage in *A Burnt-Out Case*, with the three-cornered love scene in *The Quiet American*, the chess game in *Our Man in Havana*, the prison dialogue in *The Power and the Glory*, the intrusion of Miss Paterson into the Boulogne chapters of *Travels with my Aunt*—I don't think a single book of mine has failed to give me at least once a momentary illusion of success except *The Name of Action*. When I think of the novel now I remember only my facile use of the geography of Trier, which I had first visited on my German expedition with Claud Cockburn, the echoes of my unpublished Carlist novel *The Episode* (a young man caught up idealistically in a disappointing revolution), and my discovery that a simple scene of action, a police pursuit through the night streets of Trier, was quite beyond my power to render exciting. I was failing dismally at what seemed to have come so naturally to Buchan, Haggard, Stanley Weyman. My long studies in Percy Lubbock's *The Craft of Fiction* had taught me the importance of 'the point of view' but not how to convey physical excitement.

Now I can see quite clearly where I went wrong. Excitement is simple: excitement is a situation, a single event. It mustn't be wrapped up in thoughts, similes, metaphors. A simile is a form of reflection, but excitement is of the moment when there is no time to reflect. Action can only be expressed by a subject, a verb and an object, perhaps a rhythm—little else. Even an adjective slows the pace or tranquillizes the nerve. I should have turned to Stevenson to learn my lesson: 'It came all of a sudden when it did, with a rush of feet and a roar, and then a shout from Alan, and the sound of blows and someone crying as if hurt. I looked back over my shoulder, and saw Mr. Shuan in the doorway crossing blades with Alan.' No similes or metaphors there, not even an adjective. But I was too concerned with 'the point of view' to be aware of simpler problems, to know that the sort of novel I was trying to write, unlike a poem, was not made with words but with movement, action, character. Discrimination in one's words is certainly required, but not love of one's words—that is a form of self-love, a fatal love which leads a young writer to the excesses of Charles Morgan and Lawrence Durrell, and, looking back to this period of my life, I can see that I was in danger of taking *their* road. I was only saved by failure.

The Man Within had sold 8,000 copies; *The Name of Action* barely passed a quarter of that figure. The reviewing of novels at the beginning of the thirties was at a far lower critical level than it has ever been since. Gerald Gould, a bad poet, and Ralph Strauss, a bad novelist, divided the Sunday forum between them. One was not elated by their praise nor cast down by their criticism, and the third novel which I had now begun was as false and even more derivative than *The Name of Action*.

I had left *The Times* with enough money to live on for three years, and so, to make that money go further and to give me a room in which to work, we moved into the country. We had found a thatched cottage (that pastoral Georgian dream of the industrial twenties), with a small garden and orchard, up a muddy lane on the edge of Chipping Campden. It was to rent for a pound a week (the limit of what we could afford), and we moved our few belongings there, including a newly bought Pekinese with a great passion for dustbins. There was no electric light and the Aladdin lamps smoked if we left them for a few minutes alone. We were a scared couple that first night, with no sound of accustomed traffic, only a hooting owl. After darkness fell, on the evening of our arrival, I was summoned by a knock to the back door and saw an unknown countrywoman standing outside, holding a dead rat by the tail.

'What do you want?'

'I thought yu'd be interested,' she said, swinging it to and fro.

There certainly were rats, they pattered and rustled and squeaked in the roof and they remained noisy in our thatch until a man consented to come with a ferret and drive them out. In his tight breeches with his pointed face he looked like a ferret himself—it was said in the village that he had starved his wife to death.

After a few weeks we began to lose our fear of the strange country and life became happy enough, until the future

started to cast a shadow. It was a life rich with new pleasures
—the local wines, made out of almost anything vegetable,
which could be bought from the brawny landlord Rathbone
at the Volunteer (they had no effect on the head but a great
effect on the legs), home-brewed bitter at the Noel Arms
which was kept by the stepfather of a boy called Nigel
Dennis, and an almost endless variety of walks, north,
south, east and west, to Moreton-in-Marsh and Chipping
Norton, Evesham and Broadway and Blockley and Bourton-
on-the-Water. (The Pekinese, over-exercised by fifteen-
mile walks, developed hysteria and had to be destroyed.)
There were apples from our own garden and Cos lettuces
which I had grown myself with the help of a gypsy gardener
called Buckland who came once a week and put all the snails
aside for his own supper.

The life of a village is intimate and dramatic. There is a
sense of community. People talk. In a city there may be a
suicide in the next street and you will never hear of it. It is
difficult for me to understand how I could have spent hours
with the bloodless creatures of my new novel, *Rumour at
Nightfall*, which was yet another story of the Carlist rebellion, but set this time in a Spain I had never visited. It was
as though I were unable to cut the cord which bound me to
that still-born book, *The Episode*. Didn't I sometimes in a
lucid moment measure the sentimental cardboard figures of
my fancy against the people I met every day between the
muddy lane where I lived and the Live and Let Live Inn? I
don't remember. Perhaps—even more important—I should
have measured them against my own experience, against the

memories of flight, rebellion and misery during those first sixteen years when the novelist is formed.

There had been, if I was to trust my uncle, something at least of the Greene character in *The Man Within*, if only that irrational desire to escape from himself which had led one Greene grandfather out of the Church and the other to die in St Kitts. A writer's knowledge of himself, realistic and unromantic, is like a store of energy on which he must draw for a lifetime: one volt of it properly directed will bring a character alive. There is no spark of life in *The Name of Action* or *Rumour at Nightfall* because there was nothing of myself in them. I had been determined not to write the typical autobiographical novels of a beginner, but I had gone too far in the opposite direction. I had removed myself altogether. All that was left in the heavy pages of the second was the distorted ghost of Conrad. Only once, and that at the very beginning, had the book moved with a semblance of life, when a colonel played the part of a priest and heard the confession of one of his men, dying from a wound. It was a clumsy rehearsal for a scene better rendered ten years later in *The Power and the Glory*.

3

I find in my diary of that period some of the comedy and drama of the Cotswold life which was going on all around me.

'Mass was taken by the priest from Foxcote; with a

housekeeper he lives alone in a great old house above Il-
mington, and sometimes wakes to see an owl sitting on his
bedpost. The books in the library are allowed to go to rack
and ruin for want of attention. He studies astronomy and
preaches temperance and goes about the country on a
knock-kneed horse. The landlord of the Seagrave Arms at
Weston-sub-Edge, from whom I get the parsnip wine,
serves him often with tea. According to him it is a distinction to have a knock-kneed horse. Only a good horse goes
knock-kneed.'

'A troop of strolling players, which gave performances
here the other day, apparently quarrelled at Eynsham and
divided. One family has come back here and is holding
weekly dances at the town hall for a living. Cresswell, the
rich deaf architect, who lives in the square, objected to the
noise of motor-bicycles and has forced them to stop the
dances at midnight. He tried to have moved the Wednesday
sheep market which has been held in the square for hun-
dreds of years, but in this he failed. He hunts, indeed with
fishing it is his sole amusement, and in retaliation the
farmers have warned him off their land. This is driving him
from Campden for Campden's good.'

'Father Billsborough at Mass, preaching on Missions:
"What a glorious sight! Seven thousand Zulus coming to
Communion. We don't see that in England."' (It was always
a joy to listen to Father Billsborough, the most loved man in
Campden. I remember him when he asked for money to
clean his little church, speaking of 'Millions of dead flies
breeding away on the ceiling'.)

'A lot of didicoes and travellers about, which are the local names for gypsies and tramps. A woman came to the door with a baby and a basket of clothes-pegs yesterday, and this morning at breakfast someone was singing in the lane. The tramps all seem to carry kittens with them on trolleys.'

'There was a band of pea-pickers at the station, a rough-looking man with a wooden leg, his wife (a worn, curiously refined woman) and his three children, two girls of about six and four, and a boy who could not have been more than two. We got into conversation. I found it hard to understand what the man said, but suddenly realized that he was telling me that the boy had "the smartest upper-cut since Jimmy Wilde. You go down on your knees to him and he'll give you a couple before you know where you are. Nothing can hurt that child. He fell off a hay-wagon yesterday and a car ran over his neck in Evesham once and he got up laughing." The pea-picker had once been a boxer himself and claimed to have been England's hope as a heavy-weight, but apart from his leg his hands had been ruined by labour. He held them out, calloused and trembling. "Your son will be champion instead," I suggested. "Oh," he said, "I've a better son than this, twenty-three years old, but he's lost his nerve. If the bookmakers put up one thousand pounds he wouldn't fight. He went to Birmingham against a man heavier than himself and he knocked him out so he never got up again." "They couldn't do anything to him?" I asked. "They kept him hanging about for four months, and now nothing will tempt him to fight."'

Of Charles Wade and his manor at Snowshill (Wade was a great collector of antiques with an estate in St Kitts, and he had built a remarkable model railway and village in the grounds of his manor): 'Wade, until late in the evening when nearly everybody had gone, hardly spoke at all. Bow-legged in knickerbockers and bedroom slippers with dark greying hair bobbed over his shoulders, a blue striped shirt of the "gents haberdashery" kind and a black evening tie; when he speaks he mouths his words and leaves them inchoate as though he were not used to speaking at all, and when he laughs at some rather obvious joke of a farcical physical kind he bellows like a child with open mouth. His collection is as much a toy to him as his model railway and village, and he reads nothing but Jeffery Farnol and that aloud, making appropriate noises with pieces of old iron. He can be suddenly insulting, and sitting on the floor in front of a log fire, the only light, I had a terror that he was going to insult me with a suddenness which would leave me at a loss. I lay in bed that night discussing him, and the thought of his thin walnut face and his open mouth laughing made my flesh creep.'

'In the High Street a butcher shook young living rats out of a steel cage for the fat foxhounds to eat, which sprawl with bloodshot eyes and stupid bodies on the grass gnawing bones. The villagers gathered at their doors and watched with amusement. All the way up the street I could hear the squealing of the rats.'

'Passed the lake in Northwick Park where Mrs Keiton drowned herself the other day, walking out from one of the

[205]

council houses in Broad Campden after dark on one of the bitterest nights of a cold month.'

'During breakfast the rat-catcher mysteriously appeared with a spade and a brush and cleared our path of snow, and went again before we could pay him anything. He will never ask for money, too proud to do more than accept it when proffered, though he was not too proud to starve his wife to death.'

'The old man who sells the *News of the World* on Sunday mornings was found yesterday by his wife hanging dead; he was seventy-three and Greenall, our daily, says that he could no longer stand his wife's nagging.'

'All yesterday and today Martha Hedges has been moving from her cottage to the almshouses at the other end of the village, pushing her things in an old pram, very old and pink and jaunty. Polishing her pictures on the doorstep.'

'Charley Sykes, the Campden madman, who used to parade the village heavily bearded and in rags, talking and waving his stick, has been frozen to death in his cottage at Broad Campden. Nothing in the room but a broken chair, straw where he used to sleep, and a stink. He was a gentleman, the son of a doctor; his real name was Seitz, and he is said to have gone mad from overwork during his medical examination. He was a wonderfully handsome youth and there are photographs of him in flannels with a tennis racket. He is said to have been at St John's College, Oxford. He had some money but lived in absolute squalor and begged. Fred Hart put out sixpence for him every week. The Evesham police are said once to have tried to arrest him for begging, and the story goes that he flung two policemen over a hedge. He used to walk in and out of Evesham, nine miles each way, lurching along bent almost double. Once he is said to have made his way out to India to see his relations, but they would have nothing to do with him . . . He died in the upper room of his cottage, and to get him down they put the web with which they lower coffins into the ground round his shoulders and dragged him down head first, his legs bumping on the stairs. Then they crammed him into the coffin in the clothes he wore and nailed him down. According to Greenall the fleas jumped on them from his wrists. There were sixteen pairs of boots in the cottage.'

It seems astonishing to me today that, while I was making careful notes of the vivid life around me, I was content to pursue my romantic and derivative tale to its disastrous conclusion—to publication, to the sale of only 1,200 copies, and finally to a review in a popular paper which opened my eyes at last to the worthlessness of all the work I had done till then.

4

My three guaranteed years of security had been squandered. Thanks to Peter Fleming I was reviewing novels now in the *Spectator* every fortnight, but I was deep in debt to my publishers, a debt from which I was only freed by the war ten years later—I had even had to borrow an extra twenty-five pounds to pay my income tax. If *The Man Within* had shown promise, it was the brief promise of a dud rocket on Guy Fawkes night. It made no difference to me that the review which had opened my eyes to my fool's progress was by an author, Frank Swinnerton, for whom I had little respect—I knew the truth when I read it. There was nothing for me to do but dismantle all that elaborate scaffolding built from an older writer's blue print, write it off as apprentice work and start again at the beginning. Never again, I swore, would I read a novel of Conrad's—a vow I kept for more than a quarter of a century, until I found myself with *Heart of Darkness* in a small paddle boat travelling up a Congo tributary in 1959 from one leper colony to another. I had to begin again naked, and perhaps it was for that reason I chose an adventure story, imagining it might be easier to write, a mistake difficult to understand, since I had learnt with *The Name of Action* how hard it was to make physical action simple and exciting.

I wrote the book, to the music of Honneger's *Pacific 231* on my gramophone, with a sense of doom. It is always hard for me to reread an old book, but in the case of *Stamboul Train* it is almost impossible. The pages are too laden by the anxieties of the time and the sense of failure. It was not only the two previous novels that had failed: I had wasted time and effort on a life of Lord Rochester which Heinemann had without hesitation turned down, and I was too uncertain of myself to send it elsewhere. By the time I finished *Stamboul Train* the days of security had almost run out. Even my dreams were full of disquiet—I remember how in one I was condemned to prison for five years and I woke depressed by the thought that my wife would be over thirty when we lived with each other again. The dream proved to be the germ of my next novel, *It's a Battlefield*, but I didn't realize it then, for even before *Stamboul Train* was finished I had begun to plan its successor—a novel about spiritualism and incest, with only two main characters, a fraudulent spiritualist and his sister. The sister was to move through the corruption of her surroundings failing to see that the criminality of her beloved brother had any real importance. A little of the incestuous story must have sunk back into my unconscious to emerge again four years later in *England Made Me*.

The scenes for the book were to be set in Nottingham and London. Those two cities represented the real world to me: I had done with castles in Spain, and perhaps because my decision had been made at a deeper level than the conscious, I had a dream, which I found at least half encouraging. I dreamt that I received from Heinemann an advance copy of a new novel. It was printed on bad paper; it was badly bound with a bad title, and the novel was to be published at the derisive price of ninepence. The publisher obviously cared nothing for the book, but when I opened it I had immediately the sense of strong firm writing and was saddened at the thought that in such a poor format the novel would neither be reviewed nor bought.

On August 4 I noted in my diary, 'Sent off typescript to Heinemann. Is my position at its worst? Although I have been given till September 15 to pay the remainder of my income tax, I am to all intents minus about thirty pounds, with no guarantee of any money or employment after this month.' At the end of August my contract with Heinemann and Doubleday would be over. Nearly a fortnight passed without a word from Heinemann, and I noted, 'The suspense is becoming terrible,' and, when at last the letter arrived, 'I took it half way upstairs and opened it with fingers which really trembled'. It was strange what a few words of encouragement did for me. My financial situation was still the same: the unearned royalties on my previous books would absorb any small success *Stamboul Train* might achieve. Nonetheless hope was reborn and I noted the same day a new theme for a novel which was already ousting the story of the spiritualist: 'A large inclusive picture of a city, the connecting link the conviction of a man for the murder of a policeman. Is it politic to hang him? And the detectives go out through the city listening . . .'

One ominous day I took a ticket for London to discuss the future with Charles Evans and the representative of Doubleday, my American publisher. This was Mary Pritchett, who was later to be my agent in America and one of my greatest friends. But that day she seemed a dragon indeed. Nor was I very attached to her firm. Nelson Doubleday, a tall husky man, who had once served in Roosevelt's Rough Riders and who knew more about horses than about books, would descend on London once a year and summon his authors by telegram to see him at set hours at the Heinemann office. I had received a telegram the year before. I could ill afford the ticket, but I was his pensioner and I had to go. 'Siddown,' he said, and looked at me with gloomy resentment as though

I were some underbred brute which a smart horse-dealer had swindled him into buying. He took out a handkerchief almost as huge as himself and blew his nose a number of times. 'Caught a cold coming over,' he said, and they were the only words he spoke to me. I took the next train back to Chipping Campden.

The interview with Evans and Mary Pritchett proceeded on its dreary course: accounts showing the disastrous sales of the last two books were before them: the typescript of *Stamboul Train* lay on the desk beside the accounts—the third book in the three-year contract which had now come to an end. No further advances would be due to me until another novel was completed. I waited hopelessly while an argument went on between Evans and Mary Pritchett, and then the meeting was quickly brought to a close. Heinemann, Evans said, would continue to pay me my three hundred pounds for one more year, but Doubleday would promise nothing beyond two further monthly payments, and in the meanwhile they would study the new manuscript. There were several conditions attached even to these payments—another contract for two books with all losses to be recovered by the publishers before any further royalties were paid. Only in the train back to Campden did I realize that I might have to write two novels more with no payment at all after the next year was over.

5

During the following two months, while I was still receiving payment from Doubleday, I had to find a job at all costs anywhere. Our country peace was over, and the nights held little sleep. I tried to engineer a return to *The Times* but received only Barrington-Ward's frozen response: I tried for half-time jobs on Sunday papers with no success. The *Catholic Herald* had advertised for a subeditor and again I spent the money for a ticket to London. The editor, a grey withered man who had made a name for himself as the strategical correspondent to the *Spectator*, received me with humiliating condescension. He asked for a little time to decide and I returned to the country full of hope. After two weeks he wrote asking me to come and see him again. This was certainly success, I thought, but, when I entered his room, he at once began to tell me how, with three novels to my name and my excellent experience on *The Times* behind me, he had come to the conclusion that I was too good for the job, I would never settle down. He was more condescending than ever and hardly disguised his pleasure in the interview—perhaps he hadn't liked my name appearing in the same number of the *Spectator* as his own. I had too much pride and too little spirit left to ask him to return my railway fare, and since then I have taken a biased view of Catholic journalism and Catholic humanity.

'I have been here before.' I noted in my diary the same symptoms which at sixteen used to drive me to London with my brother Raymond. They were the symptoms of a life with too little hope—then there had been frustrated love, now there was failure. 'My nerves horribly on edge; that feeling of lurking madness, of something swelling in the brain and wanting to burst; every sound, however small, made by anyone else, the clink of a plate or a fork, piercing the brain like a knife.' If there are recurrent themes in my novels it is perhaps only because there have been re-current themes in my life. Failure seemed then to be one of them.

Events took an ironic turn and convinced me of the tem-porary nature of any possible success. *Stamboul Train* was chosen by the Book Society (which meant in those days a sale of 10,000 copies) and Doubleday's consented to renew payments for another year. My immediate anxieties seemed over when: 'My God! I don't know whether to laugh or cry. A telegram from Charles Evans at eleven to ring him immediately. I do so from a call-box in the square. J. B. Priestley threatens to bring a libel action if *Stamboul Train* is published.' (I heard later that he had read a review copy sent to the *Evening Standard*.) 'The character of Mr Savory he takes for his own.' Savory, a character in *Stamboul Train*, was described as a popular novelist. He was interviewed on the Orient Express by a sadistic woman journalist who tried to make a fool of him. J. H. Thomas, the politician, was in my mind when I gave him a touch of cockney, Baldwin when I gave him a pipe—after all a popular novelist is a bit of a politician. I had never met Mr Priestley and had been unable to read *The Good Companions* which had brought him immense popularity three years before.

My suggestion that we should fight the libel action was brushed aside. Evans made it clear to me that if Heinemann were going to lose an author, they would much prefer to lose me. Thirteen thousand copies of the book had already been printed and bound. Pages would have to be substituted, and I must share the cost. Alterations had to be made at once, on the spot, without reflection.

'Charles Evans then suggests alterations on the phone, deletion of "the modern Dickens" and of all references to Dickens as he says this will appease Priestley. I am to ring up again at three-thirty and hear the result. I would laugh if all my hopes did not rest on this book.

'Rang up at 3.30. References to Dickens, to a pipe and to "blunt fingers" all to come out. Objection to the line "sold a hundred thousand copies. Two hundred characters". I had to insert a new one, on the spot, in the telephone booth. The piece of dialogue: "You believe in Dickens, Chaucer, Charles Reade, that sort of thing?" to be altered. Shakespeare must go in, instead of Dickens. And the line "Dickens will live" has to be altered to "they will live".' It was almost as though Mr Priestley were defending Dickens rather than himself.

A child was on the way, and I had only twenty pounds in the bank. My mind shifted again towards the East, as it had done when I left Oxford, and I wrote to an old Oxford friend to see whether he could fit me into his department of English at Chulankarana University near Bangkok. His favourable reply came just too late to save me from this career of writing. I had been turned back into the pen like a driven sheep by the temporary popular success of *Stamboul Train*. (How temporary it was may be judged by the fact I have already mentioned that the first printing of my first novel in 1929 was 2,500 copies and of my tenth, *The Power and the Glory*, in 1940 was 3,500.)

Twenty years later I visited my friend in Siam, as it was called then. He was still teaching in the department of English, and we smoked some opium pipes together in a little room which he had fitted up as a *fumerie* with a statue of Buddha and a couple of mattresses and a lacquer tray. At Oxford he had written poetry of great promise, but for long now he had given up any attempt to write. Unlike myself he had accepted the idea of failure and he had discovered in lack of ambition a kind of bleared happiness and an ironic amusement when he looked at his contemporaries who had found what people call success.

For a writer, I argued, success is always temporary, success is only a delayed failure. And it is incomplete. A writer's ambition is not satisfied like the business man's by a comfortable income, though he sometimes boasts of it like a *nouveau riche*. 'The reception of my *New Magdalene* was prodigious. I was forced to appear half way through the piece, as well as at the end. The acting took everyone by surprise, and the second night's enthusiasm quite equalled the first. We have really hit the mark. Ferrari translates it for Italy, Regnier has two theatres ready for me in Paris, and Lambe of Vienna has accepted it for his theatre.' Where is *The New Magdalene* now, and how many remember the name of its author?

[215]

The writer has the braggart's excuse. Knowing the un-reality of his success he shouts to keep his courage up. There are faults in his work which he alone detects; even his un-favourable critics miss them, dwelling on obvious points which can be repaired, but like a skilled intuitive builder he can sniff out the dry rot in the beams. How seldom has he the courage to dismantle the whole house and start again.

The smell of opium is more agreeable than the smell of success. We were happy that long evening, as we passed the pipe to and fro and the small flame licked upwards towards the seed of opium and the shadow moved on Buddha's fat complacent face and we talked cheerfully of the past and analysed our differing failures without guilt or regret. Hadn't Buddha failed too? The starving, the sick and the mutilated dogs lay around his temple where the yellow-robed shaven priests picked their proud way.

'Another pipe? Do you remember that awful piece of verse you wrote at Oxford about eating a Lyons' chop?'

'Oh yes, I was in love . . .'

'That excuses a lot,' he said, 'at the age you were then.'